A GUIDE FOR DEVELOPING AN INTERDISCIPLINARY THEMATIC UNIT

Patricia L. Roberts
Richard D. Kellough
California State University, Sacramento

Merrill,
an imprint of Prentice Hall

Englewood Cliffs, New Jersey   Columbus, Ohio

Library of Congress Cataloging-in-Publication Data

Roberts, Patricia
    A guide for developing an interdisciplinary thematic unit/
Patricia L. Roberts, Richard D. Kellough.
      p. cm.
    Includes bibliographical references and index.
    ISBN 0-13-326307-X (pbk.)
    1. Interdisciplinary approach in education—United States.
2. Lesson planning—United States.   I. Kellough, Richard D. (Richard Dean)
II. Title.
LB1570.R55   1996
375'.001—dc20

95-23759
CIP

Cover photo: A. Foley/H. Armstrong Roberts, Inc.
Editor: Debra Stollenwerk
Developmental Editor: Linda Ashe Montgomery
Production Editor: Julie Anderson Tober
Photo Editor: Anne Vega
Design Coordinator: Julia Zonneveld Van Hook
Text Designer: Anne D. Flanagan
Cover Designer: Scott Rattray/Rattray Design
Production Manager: Laura Messerly
Electronic Text Management: Marilyn Wilson Phelps, Matthew Williams, Karen L. Bretz,
   Tracey Ward

This book was set in New Baskerville by Prentice Hall and was printed and bound by The
Banta Company. The cover was printed by Phoenix Color Corp.

© 1996 by Prentice-Hall, Inc.
A Simon & Schuster Company
Englewood Cliffs, New Jersey 07632

Photo credits: Scott Cunningham, Cunningham/Feinknopf, p. 114; KS Studios, p. 22; Barbara Schwartz, Merrill/Prentice Hall, p. 33; Anne Vega, Merrill/Prentice Hall, pp. 14, 45,
73, 95; Tom Watson, Merrill/Prentice Hall, p. 120.

Printed in the United States of America

10 9 8 7 6 5 4 3 2 1

ISBN: 0-13-326307-X

Prentice-Hall International (UK) Limited, *London*
Prentice-Hall of Australia Pty. Limited, *Sydney*
Prentice-Hall of Canada, Inc., *Toronto*
Prentice-Hall Hispanoamericana, S. A., *Mexico*
Prentice-Hall of India Private Limited, *New Delhi*
Prentice-Hall of Japan, Inc., *Tokyo*
Simon & Schuster Asia Pte. Ltd., *Singapore*
Editora Prentice-Hall do Brasil, Ltda., *Rio de Janeiro*

Preface

In recent years, many teachers have become increasingly aware of the part an interdisciplinary thematic unit plays in determining the quality of their students' learning. Perhaps no single task will be more important in the future than that of improving our approaches to student learning. This guide provides one valuable approach and thus should serve as a supplement to what you learn in a general methods course. The sole purpose of this book is to provide guidance for developing interdisciplinary thematic units.

We believe the interdisciplinary thematic unit is an instructional strategy that will help define a new expression of our professionalism. Certainly, developing and presenting an ITU in the classroom can be challenging—this approach often tests a teacher's dedication and ingenuity. Yet, many educators hold the view that such units provide the most meaningful way to prepare students for the recreational, vocational, and everyday requirements of the twenty-first century. We predict that one of the most important challenges in the next century will be the reality of not only living life in the "fast lane" but also living life on a worldwide "information superhighway." In the year 2000 and beyond, we believe that life on the information superhighway will encompass students' interpreting their own meanings through both assigned studies and self-selected independent inquiries; that education will consist mainly of inquiry-oriented processes that require students to ask questions and to develop their thinking skills through various approaches to research and the use of diverse resources; that action-oriented students will focus on pertinent questions and issues (concepts, generalizations, theories, principles) that have not only local, regional, and state significance but also global importance; that there will be an increased emphasis on determining meaning from the interrelationships found in the content areas of various fields of study; and that integrated instructional experiences will equalize educational opportunities for all students and enhance multicultural pluralism.

We are confident that the interdisciplinary thematic approach can be useful in classrooms, though only if questioning is given the same priority that Albert Einstein gave it when reflecting upon his own learning. "The most important thing is not to stop questioning," he wrote. "Curiosity has its own reason for existing. One cannot help but be in awe when one contemplates the mysteries of eternity, of life, of the marvelous structure of reality." We believe that the interdisciplinary thematic approach can provide students with a beginning toward that "marvelous structure of reality."

Unfortunately, we are beginning to hear voices—and not merely from disgruntled critics—indicting the basic characteristics and ways of education. If we are to improve our educational approaches significantly in the years ahead, then all of us must join in making that effort. Strong action will be necessary at all educational levels. Presenting interdisciplinary thematic units in the classroom can be part of that action. In addition, private citizens and voluntary groups must join in partnerships to support the effort. This includes businesses and industries, labor and farm organizations, and scientific, health, and educational institutions—every part of our society. It is important, too, that the quality of our educational approaches continues to be seen not only as a national but also as an international concern.

To reverse a perceived deterioration in education will be one of the major goals of the next generation, involving all the main segments of society. And it will not be enough simply to cope with educational problems as they individually rise to a clear community concern about a particular problem's effect on our children's progress. As part of addressing current educational concerns, we believe that the educational progress of the future leaders of tomorrow can be assisted by an inclusion of interdisciplinary thematic units throughout the curriculum. This guide supports that proposition.

How to Use This Book

This guide is intended for any educator interested in offering, assessing, and evaluating an integrated curriculum through an interdisciplinary thematic unit. Its focus and organization is designed for teacher preparation at the college and university level, for in-service seminars and workshops at the district level, and for independent individual use. In the first four chapters, you will find helpful guidelines and ideas that will assist you in developing your own thematic units, capable of being vehicles to foster interdisciplinary awareness.

In Chapter 1, we present an explanation of the integrated curriculum and the interdisciplinary thematic unit and briefly discuss foundational theories that support the development and implementation of an ITU. In Chapter 2, we present an overview of one way to develop themes, generalizations, and a scope and sequence of learning activities for an ITU. In Chapter 3, we provide exercises to guide an interested reader in developing objectives and learning activities for an ITU. In Chapter 4, we address assessment. Although this guide cannot provide everything you might need or want to know about assessment, we do include suggestions for assessment and evaluation of students' achievement in an ITU. In Chapter 5, we offer sample ITUs that you can examine closely.

The guide also includes a reader's self-check list for an individual assessment of what was learned through the reading and the interactive exercises. In addition, there are indexes and an appendix of planning masters. The quotations from Albert Einstein at the beginning of each chapter are from *Great Quotes from Great Leaders*.

In summary, *A Guide for Developing an Interdisciplinary Thematic Unit* is intended only as a starting point for caring teachers who find themselves challenged by students who face a world with many complex problems in the near future. These students are in need of problem-solving skills that may best be developed through interdisciplinary thematic units. Although even the most committed educators cannot determine the future of students in their charge, they can provide positive role models as adults who offer and maintain interdisciplinary teaching and learning. Furthermore, teachers can enhance their curricula by accepting the students' input and placing carefully planned activities into units that will guide the students toward developing the problem-solving skills and knowledge necessary for surviving and thriving in not only today's changing times but also in the years ahead. This guide is a teacher-to-teacher discussion toward that end.

Acknowledgments

Many people helped and encouraged us during the development of this guide, although we assume full responsibility for its shortcomings. First, we want to express our warmest appreciation to the teachers who provided us with samples of materials they have developed and whose names are acknowledged within the guide. Second, we want to thank our colleagues who served as reviewers, carefully reading and reacting to the draft of this first edition: JoAnne Buggey, University of Minnesota; Barbara Kacer, Western Kentucky University; Cynthia G. Kruger, University of Massachusetts—Dartmouth; Cynthia E. Ledbetter, University of Texas at Dallas; and Linda Levstik, University of Kentucky.

Finally, we want to express our sincere appreciation to our friends at Prentice Hall: Debbie Stollenwerk, our editor, who encouraged us to write this guide and who provided intelligent technical suggestions and unfaltering emotional support throughout; Jeffrey Johnston, vice president and publisher, for his belief in and support of this project from the moment of its inception; Julie Anderson Tober, our production editor, who so expertly helped in the book's design and in moving it through the maze of production details; and to Dan Duffee, our copyeditor, who provided the needed wisdom to fine tune the manuscript.

P. L. R.
R. D. K.

Contents

Chapter 1
Introduction to an Interdisciplinary Thematic Unit   1

Chapter 2
Initiating an Interdisciplinary Thematic Unit   31

Chapter 3
Developing Objectives and Learning Activities   59

Chapter 4
Assessing and Evaluating   107

Chapter 5
Examining Thematic Units   129

Chapter

· ·

1

Introduction to an
Interdisciplinary Thematic Unit

· ·

Curiosity has its own reason for existing.

—Albert Einstein

· ·

INTERDISCIPLINARY THEMATIC UNIT FOR MIDDLE
SCHOOL STUDENTS: *THE SHUTEYES*

In 1993 Sandra Switzer, a reading consultant in the New York City schools, selected *The Shuteyes*, a novel by Mary James (Scholastic, 1993), as a way to launch an across-the-curriculum interdisciplinary study for her middle grade students, ages ten through thirteen. After careful reading, Switzer had decided that the novel was suitable for both creative and factual study from several disciplines.

In this fantasy about traveling through time, eleven-year-old Chester lives with his mother, whose activities include drum beating, chanting, and interpreting dreams for anyone who asks. Teased by his peers for his mother's behavior, Chester decides that he would rather not live with her anymore. His wish is granted when, as a time traveler, he journeys from his Mississippi home to the planet Alert. Chester struggles to adjust to life on Alert, whose inhabitants believe that sleeping is "evil" and segregate the "shuteyes" (those who fall asleep) from everyone else. Chester experiences imprisonment, isolation, brainwashing, and adoption as he attempts to adapt to a culture different from his own.

In planning this interdisciplinary unit, Switzer developed a number of creative and factual activities from the novel. These activities were related to several disciplines:

- *English.* The students discussed changes in the novel's setting, development of the plot, and the author's use of foreshadowing.
- *Expressive Arts* (reading, writing, speaking, listening, art, drama, music). The students made a model of the planet Alert and a floor plan of some of its buildings and also designed a robot similar to the novel's "Star Searcher." They also selected a section of the novel as the basis for a Reader's Theater presentation.
- *Health.* The students studied dreams and did research about sleep in humans.
- *Science.* Some students studied the flora and fauna of the state Mississippi and compared the plants and animals of New York with those in Mississippi. Other students developed an environment for the planet Alert and identified a place for it in the solar system.
- *Social Sciences.* The students engaged in a map study of Mississippi and compared New York with that state. They also developed a government for the fantasy planet, compared the segregation described in the story with real segregation happening today, and compared the freedoms of Alert's inhabitants with the freedoms of U.S. citizens as enumerated in the Bill of Rights. In addition, the students discussed important topical issues, such as prejudice and class structure.

As has become clear to many teachers, to teach the diversity of students in contemporary classes effectively, an approach that uses an integrated curriculum is best. Such an approach can prolong learning in each separate subject (discipline), in large part by making the learning more meaningful to students. This approach, as exemplified by Sandra Switzer's unit described in the opening vignette, stands in stark contrast to the teaching of separate subjects at different times during the school day. This guide is dedicated to increasing your understanding of such an integrated approach. In an integrated curriculum, subjects are intermeshed and instructional techniques are used that involve students in such socially interactive experiences as cooperative learning, cross-age tutoring, and peer tutoring. Recent research indicates that this kind of teaching can lead to high levels of thinking and meaningful learning.

As you read further about an integrated curriculum and the interdisciplinary thematic unit (ITU), in this guide and other sources, you will be confronted with a variety of terms that relate to the integration of disciplines: *integrated curriculum, interdisciplinary curriculum, thematic instruction, multidisciplinary teaching,* and *integrated studies,* among others. Regardless of the specific term used, the basic concept is the same.

This chapter has been designed to introduce you to the use of an integrated curriculum. We begin by describing the foundation that supports the development of such an approach—the major purposes, the spectrum, and the assumptions of an integrated curriculum. We then follow with specific topics related to the use of such an approach in the classroom.

A.   Major Purposes for an Integrated Curriculum

The major purposes of an integrated curriculum, consistent with the nature of children and what we as educators know about them in our classrooms, include:

1. To teach students to be independent problem solvers
2. To involve students in direct, purposeful, and meaningful learning

3. To assist students as they recognize that learning is interrelated
4. To assist students in following individual interests through individualized and personalized learning
5. To design situations in which the students learn what they want and need to know rather than what a particular curriculum indicates
6. To encourage students to work with others in cooperative learning situations, such as partnerships and small groups, that focus on the social values of learning
7. To emphasize the process of learning as whole and connected rather than as a series of specific subjects and disparate skills

B.   The Spectrum of Integrated Curriculum

The idea of an integrated curriculum is not new. From the late 1950s to the 1980s, such a curriculum was available in several different forms. Examples include the *Elementary School Science Program (ESS)*, a science program for grades K–6; *Man: A Course of Study (MACOS)*, an anthropology-based program for grade 5; and *Environmental Studies* (name changed later to *ESSENCE*), an interdisciplinary program for grades K–12. Additional programs include those based on the whole language movement in literacy/reading/language arts, programs that gained an impetus in the 1980s. Various other programs were introduced in the 1960s in middle schools and high schools, especially *Interdisciplinary Approaches to Chemistry (IAS)*, for high school chemistry. In today's schools, some teachers have embraced programs such as these, and that educational focus has been supported by successes in curriculum integration achieved in elementary, middle, and high schools across the nation (Mah, 1994; Sun, 1994). But other teachers, cognizant of small school budgets and communities that want fundamental approaches, have been critical of the integrated curriculum, especially when it seems to be permissive, unorganized, and too informal. Thus, a totally integrated curriculum may not be the best approach for every student, every teacher, and every school.

A spectrum, shown in step arrangement, should help you connect the students' learning and their experiences with the teacher's efforts in initiating an integrated curriculum (Figure 1.1). A teacher's efforts to integrate instruction can be placed somewhere on this continuum of complexity and sophistication. As you read about the different levels on the spectrum, try to identify where some of your own teaching efforts could be placed.

Level I.   The teacher plans subject-specific material in a scope-and-sequence outline that reflects a traditional organization of topics. Sometimes, the sequence includes junior high school topics (e.g., "Floods" and "The Social Effects of Natural Disasters") that could overlap or be studied at the same time, but they are not taught that way because the students have to move through the academic day from teacher to teacher. Such a traditional scope and sequence may also apply to elementary students as they receive subject-specific information at precise times during the school day—"If it's Tuesday at 8:00 a.m., it must be reading."

Level II.   The teacher uses a thematic approach as the same group of students learns material from various disciplines—science, mathematics, social studies/history, and English/language arts—during the academic day. Often, the theme, such as "Natural Disasters Cause Social Effects," originates from topics such as "Floods" and "The Social Effects of Natural Disasters." Notice that a distinction is made between a topic

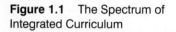

Figure 1.1   The Spectrum of
Integrated Curriculum

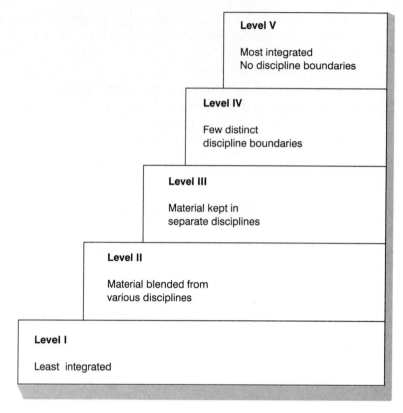

and a theme. A topic might be defined as the general subject of a study. For the purposes of this guide, a theme is defined as the point, the message, or the idea that underlies a study. The theme explains the significance of the study—it tells the students what the experience means. Many topics make up an ITU, which is organized around a theme. Often the theme of a study becomes clearer to students when an overall guiding question is presented and discussed, such as "What happens in our society after natural disasters?" Often students are encouraged to help in selecting the theme(s) and the guiding question(s), as well as choosing content to study from various disciplines.

Level III.   The teacher collaborates with other teachers on a common theme; then the teachers separately teach to that theme in their individual subject areas. This process usually occurs during an agreed-upon portion of time during the academic year. At this level, students learn from a teacher in one classroom material related to what they are learning from another teacher in another classroom. As at Level II, the students may be encouraged to help in selecting themes, guiding questions, and content.

Level IV.   The teacher collaborates with the students on a common theme and its content, making an effort to eliminate as many of the traditional boundaries between disciplines as possible. In this arrangement, the teacher can teach independently, as is often done in a self-contained classroom at an elementary school, or teach with others in a team approach, as is often done at middle and high schools when teachers can work together with a common group of students. This is the level of integrated curriculum that appears to work best for teachers in middle and secondary schools.

Level V.   The teacher collaborates with the students on a common theme and its content, with traditional boundaries between disciplines completely eliminated. A teacher may do this independently or teachers of different grade levels (e.g., sixth grade, seventh grade, and eighth grade) may work together to foster the students' understanding of different aspects from different disciplines related to a common theme. At this level, the participating teachers are all contributing to an integrated thematic approach (Stevenson and Carr, 1993).[1]

Now that you have been introduced to the levels in the spectrum, turn your attention to discussing these levels with others by completing Exercise 1.1, Reflecting Upon the Levels in the Spectrum of Integrated Curriculum. Because this guide has been prepared to assist you in developing an interdisciplinary thematic unit, it is important that you assess at which level you would feel comfortable implementing an integrated curriculum in a classroom. This initial self-assessment not only will help you become more knowledgeable about what is involved in teaching an ITU but also will help you better understand what your professional relationship with other teachers and with the students might be like.

EXERCISE 1.1

Reflecting upon the Levels in the Spectrum of Integrated Curriculum

• • • • • •

Instructions.   The purpose of this exercise is to share with others (perhaps in small groups according to grade levels) your reflections about the levels at which you see yourself teaching in the spectrum of integrated curriculum.

1. At which levels do you see yourself teaching? Why?

2. Which levels do you see yourself avoiding? Why?

3. What do you see as some of the professional relationships you will have with other teachers and with the students?

Notes during group discussion:

C.   Assumptions for an Integrated Curriculum

The theoretical foundation for an integrated curriculum can be found in student inquiry (Beyer, 1985; Costa, 1985), class management in an atmosphere of active inquiry (Harmin, 1994), schema theory (Bruner, 1986; Vygotsky, 1978, and Wells, 1986), the whole language approach (Goodman, 1986), and a related model of learning (Caine and Caine, 1993). All of these lend support to the idea that using an interdisciplinary thematic unit is a valuable, reflective, and effective way to teach students. Furthermore, Goodman and his colleagues have found the roots of the whole language approach in the philosophy of John Dewey, the early twentieth-century educator. In *Language and Thinking in School* (1987), they assert that whole language is built upon Dewey's work.

Inquiry

When involved in inquiry—seeking knowledge by asking questions, investigating, and searching for information—the teacher recognizes that the students bring natural interests, drives, and urges to school with them every day. The teacher actively explores those student interests and backgrounds, perhaps beginning with a teacher-developed student interest inventory or with the use of the technique known as think-pair-share.[2] And from that exploration, the teacher can elicit and develop significant learning activities. Throughout this process, the teacher often assumes the roles of adviser, facilitator, and guide. To complement the natural way that students explore, the process may incorporate a flexible time schedule and non–subject specific periods of time, with little or no traditional curriculum components. The students become involved in many opportunities that foster cooperation and social integration. They work with one another in partnerships and small groups to explore their interests and to learn from experiences related to their interests. In some classrooms, the teacher encourages cross-age grouping, involving older students in activities. Cross-age grouping or tutoring provides an avenue for self-esteem to be developed in older students as they assist the younger ones. When implemented by the teacher, these practices, which tend to support an integrated curriculum, contribute to a stimulating classroom environment suitable for student learning.

Class Management in an Atmosphere of Active Inquiry

When children are actively learning, they are exactly that—active. And when children are active they can be noisy, even boisterous. Most certainly they are noisier than when in the traditional classroom, in which all students are seated with their chairs facing the front of the room in which the teacher spends much of his or her time doing teacher-centered instruction. When actively learning via an ITU, though, the movements and noise made by students are more likely to be educationally necessary movements and productive noises. When a student's movement or noise is not necessary or enhancing to the learning activity, then—just as when using any other type of instructional strategy—the teacher must implement his or her usual management plan, thereby reminding the student of procedures and if necessary applying the consequences of not following those procedures.

To implement ITUs successfully, which necessarily involves the learners in active learning, sometimes requires a shift in the teacher's concept of classroom management and control. Integrated studies require students to take more responsibility for their own learning and for their own conduct. Much less class time is spent in teacher-centered, work-sheet-oriented, and textbook-oriented instruction. Thus, for teachers who have difficulty sharing authority with their students, an approach that incorporates active inquiry means confronting in new ways what has traditionally been referred to as control and discipline. An emphasis on student initiative and responsibility produces a much greater frequency of those teachable moments that mean so much to both students and adults. Because ITUs usually take on a life of their own, students also assume responsibility for their own lives more willingly. They like having the trust and independence to be more responsible for themselves. Prudent teachers regularly restructure grouping patterns according to students' needs to work in a variety of group roles and to the requirements of particular activities.[3]

Schema Theory

Schema theory holds that a student's schema consists of mental representations of knowledge and that a student often faces cognitive challenges that cause changes in that schema (Bruner, 1986, Vygotsky, 1978, Wells, 1986). When this happens, a student's knowledge can be restructured in specific domains (Smith, 1983). For example, a teacher can foster opportunities for cognitive challenges in learning through the integrative approach of an interdisciplinary thematic unit—when the perspectives of various disciplines themselves offer unique and unusual challenges.

How schemata are constructed and changed is not fully understood. There is a need for more information about the students' cognition and about different cultural schemata to help guide various teaching practices further. Currently, we suspect that different cultural schemata may affect the mental representations of knowledge for various students, but as of now we realize we don't know enough about this aspect of schema theory (Lee, 1989). Perhaps this is an area you'll be interested in pursuing in your own classroom research.

Whole Language Approach

From schema theory also comes support for the concept of whole language as a set of beliefs about how learning happens (Moffett & Wagner, 1983) as well as a set of principles to guide teaching practices in the classroom (Goodman, 1986). Advocates of whole language learning assert that each student is an active, constructive learner who uses his or her language for social reasons (Bates, 1976) and in doing so organizes and constructs the language that is needed (Trevarthan, 1979). Through organizing and constructing language, a student builds on prior schema and forms hypotheses about how oral and written language operates (Smith, 1983). In the process, the student classifies his or her experiences (Halliday, 1982) and learns through his or her language (Bruner, 1983). For example, as a student learns about writing, he or she gains the ability to express his or her schema through written language (Kagan, 1972; Rosenblatt, 1978, 1983). When a student reads and gains understandings, the student comes to the realization that reading a text is quite different from speaking (Smith, 1981, 1983; Wells, 1981, 1985). When a student compares a reading text with speaking, the student can face additional conflicts, because the situation, context, and linguistics can be quite different—and those conflicts affect the student's schema.

From the concept of whole language learning comes educational support for the notion that the expressive arts—speaking, listening, reading, writing—should be learned in authentic speech and literacy events (Newman, 1985). Thus, authentic events that incorporate the expressive arts can foster a student's language development, which in turn relies on a student's cognitive development, or schemata (Wells, 1985).

A Model of Meaningful Learning

The educators Geoffrey Caine and Renate Nummela Caine (1993) have translated research on how the brain works into practical applications for the classroom. They point out that an important goal for teachers is to assist students in relating to, or connecting with, the different parts of the curriculum. Caine and Caine advocate techniques and strategies that generate a sense of connectedness in the students' thinking and also emphasize that a teacher needs to monitor the students' sense of connectedness. They suggest that students should be involved in authentic experiences that involve group participation in genuine community problems in order to help students engage in the use of natural language and natural movement. They also emphasize that students should be engaged in peer and other relationships as well as physical movements from place to place in order to trigger the memory system, which responds to novelty and automatically maps where students are in space.

Caine and Caine point out that teachers should strive for an educational environment in which students can gain new insights and confront confusion and uncertainty. Additionally, teachers should be aware of students who might perceive learning as a threat, engendering feelings of helplessness or causing a difficulty in perceiving new opportunities. Some students have difficulty in recognizing context cues or dealing with uncertainty. Other students have difficulty accessing ideas and procedures that they already know. This set of difficulties that students experience, known as "downshifting," is discussed at length in *Human Brain, Human Learning* by Les Hart, who discusses these difficulties at greater length. Downshifting needs to be minimized if teachers want students to learn for meaning, and Caine and Caine make several suggestions about how to accomplish that during instruction:

1. Keep outcomes relatively open-ended, and make several solutions possible.
2. Maximize personal meaning by treating students as individuals and fully considering their life experiences and understandings.
3. Keep students participating by building upon their intrinsic motivation.
4. Acknowledge that students develop at different rates and that learning and change are developmental processes by incorporating tasks that have relatively open-ended time lines.
5. Keep the learning tasks manageable and related to appropriate degrees of difficulty as well as available resources.

Interdisciplinary Learning

From Caine and Caine's model of meaningful learning, as well as from the concepts of inquiry, schema theory, and whole language, comes an overall understanding that valuable student learning can be supported by an integration of the curriculum. To nurture what students learn through an integrated curriculum, the teacher can initiate units that include use of knowledge—a use that has an origin—from various disciplines. The teacher's interaction with the students might also include developing graphics such as schema (word) maps, incorporating collaborative learning, encouraging a risk-taking environment, and developing hypotheses. The students can "reserve" topics for individual inquiry and respond to peer and teacher feedback.

Students' Schema Maps.   One example of an interactive strategy is the use of students' schema (word) maps, which can be introduced by the teacher as a way to get a visual account of the students' knowledge. Schema maps (concept maps) are graphic webs that students prepare, often at intervals throughout the unit, to provide a visual account of each student's schema at a given time in the study (Lindfors, 1987; Wells, 1981). Planning Master 1 illustrates a graphic web with spaces for the students' words to indicate what they know about a topic or theme. After demonstrating with the example, a teacher might ask for pre-unit and post-unit schema maps (as well as periodic ones) to be prepared by the students. A review of the maps will help in assessing student growth related to a topic or subtopic in the unit. (See the Appendix for planning masters. The first eight planning masters in the Appendix should prove useful as transparencies for overhead-projector use in your group and, where appropriate, with students. The remaining planning masters are duplicates of exercises in the text and are included at the request of educators who wanted duplicates as guides to use when future ITUs were developed.)

To explore your own schemata related to an ITU, do Exercise 1.2, Brainstorming Ideas Related to an ITU. This exercise will help you in developing a list of topics related to a unit of study.

A diverse group of students work together in a warm, friendly, and accepting environment.

EXERCISE 1.2

Brainstorming Ideas Related to an ITU

• • • • • •

Instructions.   With others in a small group, brainstorm ideas related to an interdisciplinary thematic unit and offer suggestions. Your purpose is to develop a list of topics related to a theme or topic of your choice. Remember, there are no right or wrong ideas—all are accepted. Consider the suggestions in the following web to keep the brainstorming going if the ideas lag.

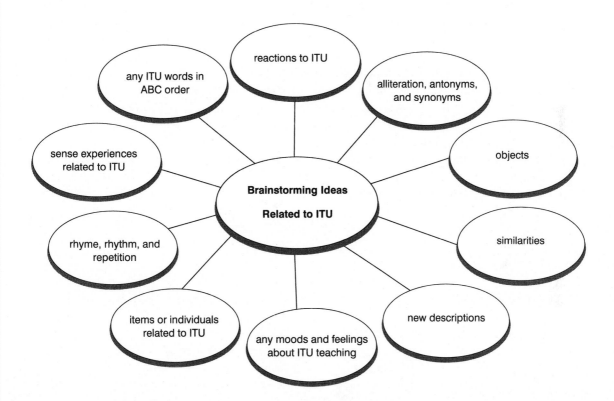

Involve two volunteers from the group to record your group's ideas on a chart or on a transparency that can be shown to others in the class on the overhead projector. You can organize the ideas in a web or another format as you wish. Follow these steps in completing the exercise:

1. Suggest ways to categorize ideas about developing an interdisciplinary thematic unit and then suggest a theme and headings for the categories you see in the web included in this exercise.

2. Individually, locate one professional article about an interdisciplinary thematic unit and read it. Take notes.

3. Return to your small group and add any information to the web that you gained from the article.

4. Meet back with the whole group and report on the group's ideas about the interdisciplinary thematic unit. Note the similarities and the differences in the schemata among the groups. Use the space that follows for your notes (if needed).

D.   Role of the Teacher in an Integrated Curriculum

When initiating an integrated curriculum, the teacher wants to provide a warm, friendly, and accepting environment in which the students can freely engage in learning activities that relate to their own interests, needs, and abilities. Specialists have pointed out that the more diverse the students, the more integrated the curriculum should be (Garcia, 1994). In this integration, a single theme should be the organizational focus of both the language activities and the various content areas (disciplines such as math and science). The teacher needs to provide ways for students to study a topic in depth and to develop a variety of skills. The teacher needs to be resourceful and open to suggestion in order to build upon the interests of the students. To do this, the teacher will want to have an assortment of classroom learning materials for the students to touch, manipulate, explore, and experiment with. Furthermore, the teacher will want to take advantage of all of the school-related learning related to the activities. Through it all, the teacher must act as a catalyst who can stimulate the learning of the students as they explore issues that mean something to their lives. For example, the teacher might help students compare a community of ancient Greece with their own community. As they explore, the students themselves will stimulate one another and will help the teacher, too, become a learner.

Teaching a Diversity of Students

Researchers Dwyer (1991), Villegas (1991), Tikunoff (1983) and others have emphasized the qualities of effective teachers—especially those who work with culturally diverse students. In the research, being *effective* was defined as (1) having teaching behaviors that produced rates of academic learning as high as or higher than the rates reported in previous research on effective teaching and (2) being seen as effective in delivery of instruction and organization by other teachers and school personnel as well as by students and parents.

Research related to a teacher's knowledge, skills, disposition, and feelings and emotions indicate that effective teachers of culturally and linguistically diverse students are those who

- Possess the ability to communicate rationales for instructional techniques and participate in staff development through courses and workshops (*knowledge*)
- Demonstrate specific instructional skills (e.g., organize instruction so it is meaningful to students), incorporate hands-on active learning, use patterned books for reading, plan lessons around individual skills, encourage collaborative and cooperative interactions among students, and use a thematic curriculum in consultation with the students (*skills*)
- Specify task outcomes and pass along their high expectations of student success (i.e., what students must do to accomplish tasks) (*skills*)
- Communicate clearly when giving directions and presenting new information (*skills*)
- Engage students in instruction by pacing instruction appropriately, by involving the students in the lessons through collaborative and cooperative learning, by monitoring the progress of the students, and by providing prompt feedback (*skills*)
- Mediate instruction for limited-English-proficient (LEP) students by alternately using both the students' native language and English for instruction, thus providing clarity (*skills*)

- Seek help from others and provide help when asked; describe themselves as confident, creative, energetic, resourceful, and collaborative; and spend their own money to get the materials the students needed (*disposition*)
- Believe that classroom practices that tend to validate the diverse cultural and linguistic heritages of students are important ways of fostering self-esteem in students (*feelings and emotions*)
- Believe that multicultural awareness enriches the lives of all students (e.g., learning about Latino culture not only benefits Latino students but also helps develop a sensitivity to another culture in other students) (*feelings and emotions*)

Various teacher interactions, a number of which are shown in Figure 1.2, can be suitably integrated into an interdisciplinary thematic unit (Planning Master 2 will be helpful in preparing an overhead transparency for a group discussion). What other interactions for the classroom teacher would you add to the diagram? What examples would you place under the headings?

E.   Role of the Students in an Integrated Curriculum

In an integrated curriculum, the emphasis should be on the cooperation, responsibility, and initiative that students demonstrate in the activities and throughout the learning process. This emphasis should be at the center of the students' involvement in their learning. For example, in various learning activities students will be expected to work with others in partnerships and small groups. Membership and roles within groups will vary, depending both on the activity and on each student's interest. As part of that interest, an individual student can "reserve" a particular topic of study. The student then searches for answers to questions that he or she has asked, in consultation with the teacher. The student's search may include moving around the classroom, asking questions, consulting others, and referring to data sources of their choice that are appropriate, suitable, and meaningful.

Various student interactions, a number of which are shown in Figure 1.3, can be suitably integrated into an interdisciplinary thematic unit (Planning Master 3 will be helpful in preparing an overhead transparency for group discussion). What other student interactions would you add to the diagram? What examples would you place under the headings?

Figure 1.2   Web of Teacher Interactions

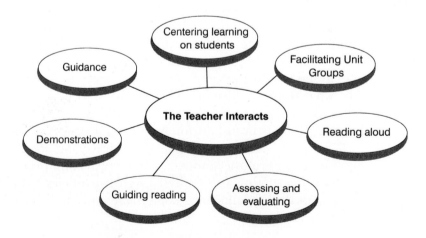

Figure 1.3   Web of Student
Interactions

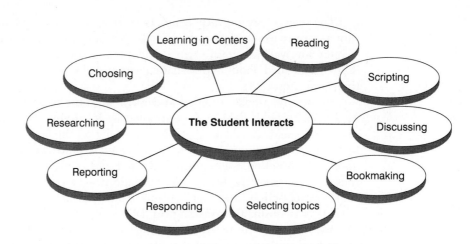

F.   Role of Technology and Media in an Integrated Curriculum

When using ITUs, technology and media are relied upon as valuable sources of information (e.g., CD-ROMs, electronic field trips, videos), as instruments for organizing and making sense of data (e.g., computer software and graphic calculators), and as vehicles for sharing information (e.g., systems for telecommunications).

For example, what began in 1992 as an isolated, single-grade, telecommunications-dependent project for sixth graders at West Salem Middle School (Wisconsin) eventually developed into a cross-grade interdisciplinary program of students and adults working together to design and develop a local nature preserve. In the words of Jan Wee, Media Director of the West Salem Middle School:

> During the spring of 1992, sixth graders began their adventure by interacting with explorer Will Steger as he led the International Arctic Project's first training expedition. Electronic on-line messages, via the Internet network, allowed students to receive and send messages to Will and his team in real time. Students delved into the Arctic world, researching the physical environment and the intriguing wildlife, reading native stories and novels about survival, keeping their own imaginary expedition journals, learning about the impact of industrialized society on the Arctic, and conversing with students from around the world. But something very important was missing—a connection between the students' environment and the faraway Arctic.
>
> For the past two summers [1992 and 1993], the World School's International Design Team has met to further develop the program. The common theme of connecting the Arctic to the local schools has been discussed again and again. Design team members agree that study projects should be developed to facilitate the philosophy of "Think Globally, Act Locally." If students can understand their local environment, they can better understand how their local actions impact the entire globe.
>
> West Salem's focus became the local 700-acre Lake Neshonoc, an impoundment of the LaCrosse River, a tributary of the Mississippi. Students had never formally studied the lake, although many have enjoyed its recreational opportunities. The Neshonoc Partners, a committee of parents, community leaders, teachers, students, and environmentalists, was established to assist in setting goals, brainstorming ideas, and developing the program for the year's study of the lake.
>
> Right from the start, students showed keen interest in active involvement in the project. A second committee, involving parents, students, and the classroom teacher, met during lunch time on a weekly basis to allow for more intensive discussions about the lake and the overall project.

The team of sixth grade teachers brainstormed ideas to further develop an interdisciplinary approach to the study of Lake Neshonoc. Special activities, including an all-day "winter survival" adventure, gave students a sense of what the real explorers experience. Students learned about hypothermia, winter trekking by cross-country skiing, and building their own snow caves.

For several weeks in April and May, students learned about the ecosystem of Lake Neshonoc through field experiences led by local environmentalists and community leaders. Guest speakers told their stories about life on the lake and their observations about the lake's health. Student sketchbooks provided a place to document personal observations about the shoreline, water testing, animal and plant life, and the value of the lake. From these sketchbooks, the best student creations were compiled to create books to share with their project-circle member schools from Russia, Canada, Missouri, South Carolina, Nevada, Wisconsin, and Washington, DC.

The opportunity to share findings about their local watershed sparked discussions about how students can make a difference in their own community. Comparative studies gave students a chance to consider how other watersheds are impacted by man and nature.

West Salem students worked with the LaCrosse County Parks and Recreation Department to assist in developing a sign marking the new County Park where the nature sanctuary will reside. Students brainstormed design ideas and then constructed the beautiful redwood sign with the help of technical educational teacher John Howe. Today the sign is a symbol of the partnership that has been established between the students and the community. It is a concrete reminder that together we can work for the common good of the community and the environment.

Students celebrated the study of the lake with a closure event on June 3, 1993. Will Steger, along with community leaders, parents, school board members, and staff, commended the students for what is sure to be the start of a long and enduring relationship—a partnership created out of common respect and appreciation for the value of our ecosystem.[4]

A school in Hamburg, Germany, provides another good example. Arctic Yearbook 1994 is an international, cross-curricular project for secondary level students of English as a foreign language (EFL). In Hamburg, teachers of biology, math, history, German, and English work with a class of students, using as a central theme the development of plankton. The goal is to gradually enlarge the students' perspective from the school's own pond to the river Elbe, to the North Sea, and to the Northern Atlantic Ocean. The 1994 plan involved contacting the Bremerhaven-based Alfred Wegener Institute, which is conducting research near Greenland, and establishing telecommunications with the Institute's research vessel *Polarstern*. During the thematic study the sixteen-to-eighteen-year-old students will develop their understandings in biology, math, history, and language.

G.   About Diversity and Multiculturalism

Today, most teachers realize that students comprise a great diversity of individuals, with a full range of cultural, ethnic, and economic heritage and first languages. Teachers must realize that America's people are multi-everything—multilingual (features of language) and multiethnic and multicultural (our features of customs, religion, traditions, history). Thus, the students in U.S. classrooms represent the changing demographics of a pluralistic nation.

Every teacher should want to improve the quality of human relations in the classroom, to foster an appreciation in students for the multiethnic composition of our society, to help them become aware of who they are as individuals and who they are as

Americans—for they have all had an American experience. An interdisciplinary thematic unit can be a good vehicle for improving the quality of human relations in the classroom, especially when it includes projects designed to provide a multicultural perspective. Such projects can help students understand the idea of *e pluribus unum* ("out of many, one"), enriching their sense of the tremendous variety of American experiences and what being an American means to each individual American.

Several projects are shown in Figure 1.4, which focuses on diversity and multiculturalism. Ironically, to show the many interdisciplinary possibilities, the different areas had to be sectioned apart instead of integrated into a whole.

H.   Initiating an Interdisciplinary Thematic Unit

When initiating an interdisciplinary thematic unit, the teacher will want to plan parts of the unit in advance, and will also want to make changes in the unit as the students' study evolves, as their interests become known and their input is included. The essential steps in developing a unit, some of which are discussed in more detail in later chapters, include:

1. Locate the available instructional resources that might be needed.
2. Write the unit overview (summary), goals, and instructional objectives.
3. Select and organize the subject matter, including writing some overall questions, and then develop problems, experiences, and activities (e.g., constructing, discussing, drawing, evaluating, experimenting, listening, observing, organizing, performing drama roles, sharing, traveling on field trips).
4. Build upon the curiosity of the students about the theme when starting a unit.
5. Arrange the class environment with materials that will interest and stimulate the students to want to know more about the theme.
6. Plan a finale to close the unit, and engage students in summarizing what they have learned with other students or with their parents or other community members.
7. Plan appropriate assessment procedures throughout the unit.

I.   Use of Instructional Resources and the Community

In an integrated curriculum, a wide variety of learning materials are needed to help make the environment rich and responsive for students. Such materials should be those that can satisfy the learning needs of the students, who are responsible for their own learning. These materials might include both familiar sources—art supplies, audiovisual materials, books, computers, CD-ROMs—as well as materials perhaps unfamiliar to some students—certain artifacts, almanacs, construction kits, and discarded household items that can be taken apart and repaired (e.g., alarm clocks, coffee pots, etc.). Other sources include films, filmstrips, recordings, pictures, maps, science equipment, tools, terrariums, math manipulatives, and scales and other measurement items.

Using the Community as a Resource

Community members, geographic features, buildings, monuments, historic sites, and other places in the local area constitute one of the richest instructional laboratories

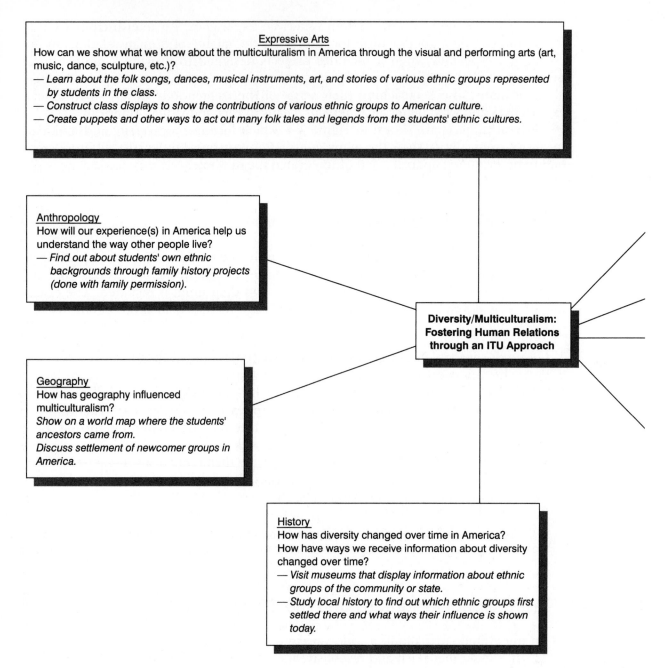

Figure 1.4   Activity Web

that can be imagined. In order to take advantage of this accumulated wealth near your school, as well as to build school-community partnerships, you should start collecting an index file of community resources that could support the interests of the students and your instruction. For instance, you might include file cards about the skills of the students' parents and other family members, noting which ones could be resources for the study occurring in your classroom. You might also include file cards on various resource people who could speak to the class, on free and inexpensive materials, and on sites for field trips related to classroom study. You might want to explore additional sources in articles in your newspaper and in the yellow pages of your area's telephone directory (Chapter 2 discusses more about the community as a resource).

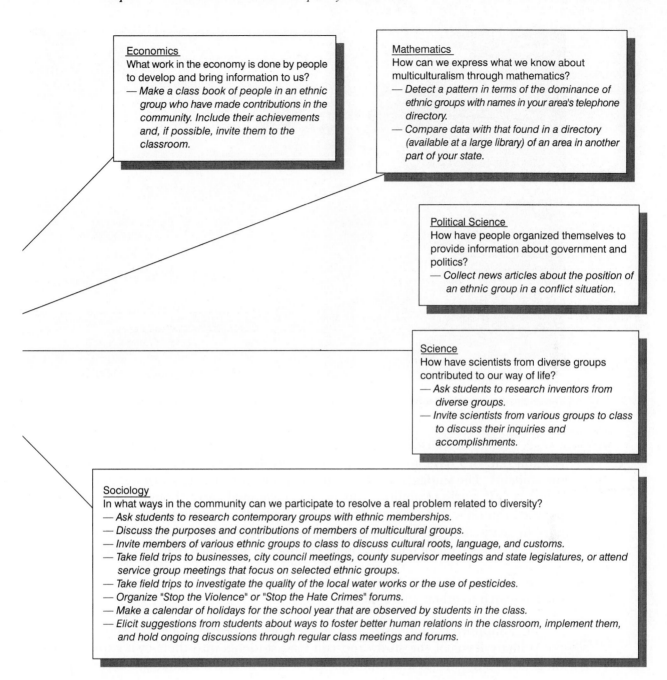

Economics
What work in the economy is done by people to develop and bring information to us?
— *Make a class book of people in an ethnic group who have made contributions in the community. Include their achievements and, if possible, invite them to the classroom.*

Mathematics
How can we express what we know about multiculturalism through mathematics?
— *Detect a pattern in terms of the dominance of ethnic groups with names in your area's telephone directory.*
— *Compare data with that found in a directory (available at a large library) of an area in another part of your state.*

Political Science
How have people organized themselves to provide information about government and politics?
— *Collect news articles about the position of an ethnic group in a conflict situation.*

Science
How have scientists from diverse groups contributed to our way of life?
— *Ask students to research inventors from diverse groups.*
— *Invite scientists from various groups to class to discuss their inquiries and accomplishments.*

Sociology
In what ways in the community can we participate to resolve a real problem related to diversity?
— *Ask students to research contemporary groups with ethnic memberships.*
— *Discuss the purposes and contributions of members of multicultural groups.*
— *Invite members of various ethnic groups to class to discuss cultural roots, language, and customs.*
— *Take field trips to businesses, city council meetings, county supervisor meetings and state legislatures, or attend service group meetings that focus on selected ethnic groups.*
— *Take field trips to investigate the quality of the local water works or the use of pesticides.*
— *Organize "Stop the Violence" or "Stop the Hate Crimes" forums.*
— *Make a calendar of holidays for the school year that are observed by students in the class.*
— *Elicit suggestions from students about ways to foster better human relations in the classroom, implement them, and hold ongoing discussions through regular class meetings and forums.*

Figure 1.4   *continued*

J.   Advantages and Limitations of an Integrated Curriculum

During the past few years, suggestions for using interdisciplinary thematic units have been made by many educators, who have emphasized that this type of unit is a highly effective educational approach. Educators interested in using this approach agree on several points about its advantages:

1.   Advocates point to inquiry, schema theory, whole language learning, and models of the brain and learning to support the practical application of an integrated curriculum as an avenue of active learning for today's students.

These children are taking advantage of a superb community resource, the zoo.

2.   Some supporters applaud the educational variety central to an integrated curriculum—no two days are ever the same, and the curriculum changes depending on the students. The students become active participants in their learning, not just passive listeners. All levels of abilities can be acknowledged. And though the curriculum is planned carefully, it is open-ended. These supporters emphasize that an interdisciplinary thematic unit enables teachers to serve a large number of students and use students' classroom research to determine changes in approach that will enhance learning.

3.   Some advocates mention that teachers will be able to pass on the success of their research to others more quickly.

4.   Supporters emphasize that the teacher can easily elicit the students' ideas as the primary focus of the study and can lead students into their own explorations, as the teacher stays within the requirements of school, district, and state documents.

5.   Supporters suggest that using an ITU makes large themes and related concepts manageable for students. One early advocate of this approach, Philip H. Phenix of Columbia University, maintained that knowledge did not have to become more and more complicated as one went deeper into a discipline but that knowledge could have its "simplicities" (Massialas and Hurst, 1978). As examples of this, Phenix mentions two scientists who discovered "simplicities" by delving deep into their respective disciplines: "how much simpler Copernicus made the understanding of the apparent motions of the stars, and planets, and how much easier Darwin made the comprehension of the varieties of living things!"

6.   Advocates seem to be in accord that teachers and students can best meet their varied needs in different environments through ITUs. Indeed, some maintain that the more diverse the students, the more integrated the curriculum should be.

7. Advocates seem to be in accord that the use of an ITU will attract support and needed resources from the school and the district.

Those are some of the points made by educators who say "yes" to the use of an interdisciplinary thematic unit as an approach to teaching and learning. Now consider the points of those who say "no." Here are what some experts consider to be limitations:

1. Not all educators believe there is adequate time or resources to plan and implement an ITU in every classroom. One common problem that could arise in developing an ITU is finding common planning time for several teachers. These critics also believe that some resources related to certain disciplines are of questionable value and are often boring.

2. Not all educators, especially first and second-year teachers, are comfortable with the idea that there is no manual of instructions to follow that could provide the themes, connections, metaphors, stories, and other materials to help integrate the learning; that there is additional distractive movement and noise that might be detrimental to the learning of some students; and that assessment strategies are difficult to design.

3. Not all educators believe that an ITU is effective in the classroom with all students. Related to this, another problem could arise when a predeveloped ITU is used in which the students don't have an opportunity to participate. Such a unit might positively affect the learning of only a limited number of students.

4. Not all educators believe that an ITU approach contributes to research, because the student population in any one classroom may not be representative and thus the benefits seemingly accrued would not be transferable to other classrooms.

5. Not all educators believe that an ITU is easy to implement. Successful class management and control may become difficult, with additional movement and noise built into the integrated curriculum. An ITU might be difficult to plan and implement because of the restraints on resources and time generated from the home, the community, the classroom, the school, and the district. For example, there is no agreed-upon structure, scope and sequence, content, or time regulation for study across the disciplines through the grade levels.

6. Not all educators believe that the approach would be accepted by a majority of students, parents, and teachers. For example, an ITU would require a great deal of time for a teacher's prior planning as well as a willingness and interest by all in implementing it in the classroom. Additionally, it would require that a teacher understand the theory and philosophy behind such a unit in order to implement the interdisciplinary feature effectively.

7. Not all educators believe that teachers know where the students are in terms of knowledge and skills—some teachers lack the imagination to predict how students at different grade levels could benefit through an ITU. Not all educators believe that the students who direct their own learning will challenge their own assumptions to gain accurate concepts and principles. As a consequence, those students will retain inaccurate concepts and principles.

Summary

This chapter has provided an introduction to developing an interdisciplinary thematic unit (ITU) and has addressed the levels on the Spectrum of Integrated Curriculum. To provide a foundation for using an ITU, a brief review of the related theory has been provided, and some advantages and disadvantages of using ITUs have been presented. Chapter notes and questions for discussion are provided at the end of this chapter. To help you further reflect upon this chapter, complete one or both of the following exercises—Exercise 1.3, Discovering Informational Sources about Interdisciplinary Thematic Units, and Exercise 1.4, Interviewing a Teacher about Interdisciplinary Thematic Units.

EXERCISE 1.3

Discovering Informational Sources About ITUs

• • • • • •

Instructions.   You have an important responsibility to be knowledgeable about an integrated curriculum before you develop an interdisciplinary thematic unit for your students. What informational sources stand out as useful ones in your mind? Your educational purpose for this exercise is to record some of the sources you can locate from your college studies that will help you in developing an interdisciplinary thematic unit around a theme you have selected. Share what you have found with others in your class. One of your sources might be just the one someone else needs to develop and implement a unit. For example, a search through the most recent edition of *Children's Books in Print* and *Subject Guide to Children's Books in Print* (both annually published by Bowker) will help you identify literature for children as a resource for a particular ITU.

   If you need assistance in locating a source that provides the information you want, select an entry from the Suggested Readings at the end of this book.

1. Source:

   Reason selected:

2. Source:

   Reason selected:

3. Source:

   Reason selected:

4. Source:

   Reason selected:

5. Source:

   Reason selected:

6. Source:

   Reason selected:

7. Source:

   Reason selected:

8. Source:

   Reason selected:

EXERCISE 1.4

Interviewing a Teacher about ITUs

• • • • • •

Instructions. For this exercise, interview one or more elementary, middle, or high school teachers. Perhaps you will want to interview one who is new to the profession and then interview one who has been in teaching for five years or more. As an option, you may want to interview one who is teaching in elementary school and one who is teaching either at the middle school or high school. For this exercise, you should make blank copies of this form. Use the questions to guide the interview, and then report back to the whole group.

1. In what ways do you use interdisciplinary thematic units?

2. Why are you using (not using) interdisciplinary thematic units?

3. What training about interdisciplinary thematic units did you have?

4. What initial advice in terms of preparing an interdisciplinary thematic unit can you offer me?

5. In what ways do you use resources in the community?

6. In what ways do you address the importance of diversity and multiculturalism in your classroom?

7. What do you like most about teaching with an interdisciplinary thematic unit? the least?

8. What other specific advice do you have for those of us developing interdisciplinary thematic units?

9. Other notes:

Chapter Notes

1. The section entitled Spectrum of Integrated Curriculum was developed by Richard D. Kellough and appears in a similar form in several Prentice Hall books in concurrent production (1995 and 1996 copyrights).
2. For example, when introducing a new topic or concept, the teacher writes on the board. Students are then paired and asked to discuss what meaning the words have, generating experiences or thoughts they have about the topic and not being concerned about whether they are right or wrong. After sharing their ideas in pairs—and perhaps writing their ideas (i.e., think-write-pair-share)—the pairs then share their thoughts with the rest of the class. The teacher records these thoughts and experiences on the board and then builds lessons from those shared thoughts and experiences. For further elaboration on this and other techniques for motivating and inspiring active learning, see M. Harmin, *Inspiring Active Learning: A Handbook for Teachers* (Alexandria, VA: Association for Supervision and Curriculum Development, 1994).
3. Chris Stevenson and Judy F. Carr (eds.), *Integrated Studies in the Middle Grades* (New York: Teachers College Press, 1993), p. 198.
4. Jan Wee, "The Neshonoe Project: Profiles in Partnership," *World School for Adventure Learning Bulletin* (Fall 1993):2–3. Reprinted by permission.

Questions and Activities for Discussion

1. What classroom observations and experiences have your peers had related to the use of ITUs in the classroom? Ask them to share their observations with you in small-group or whole-class discussions. Take notes on the discussion and, with the group members, suggest any guidelines for teaching with ITUs you infer from those notes.
2. What questions do you have about developing ITUs? Offer your questions to peer volunteers to write on a question map on the board, on an overhead transparency, or on a large sheet of butcher paper. Copy the final question map and use one of the questions to start your own individual inquiry about ITUs. Report what you find to others in a group meeting.
3. Read a current or recent article in the professional literature about the disciplinary advocates who would draw the topics or themes for thematic study from such sources as the Bradley Commission. To give yourself a contrasting view, also read an article about the social studies advocates who would draw the topics for thematic study from such sources as the National Council of Social Studies Standards, the NCSS History Standards, and curriculum frameworks in *Social Education*. Report what you learned from the articles in a small-group or whole-class discussion.
4. Some critics have serious concerns about the kinds of thematic units discussed in much of the literature currently available. For example, one concern is that the in-depth studies on ITUs may be about topics that are neither meaningful nor personally and academically powerful to learner and teacher. If this concern is expressed by a parent, in what way(s) would you assure the parent that the selected topic(s) has personal and academic value for the children?
5. Support for developing and implementing ITUs is available in educational theory, especially that related to constructivism; see, for example, Jacqueline Grennon Brooks and Martin G. Brooks, *In Search of Understanding: The Case for Constructivist Classrooms*

(Alexandria, VA: Association for Supervision and Curriculum Development, 1993). Support is also found in inquiry, schema theory, the whole language approach, and testimonials of classroom experiences and research. Related to theory, research, and practice on this topic, volunteer to report on one or more of the entries in the bibliography (see back of the guide) to a small group or to the entire class.

6. Do you agree or disagree with the major purposes for using an integrated curriculum put forth in this chapter? State your reasons for agreeing or disagreeing. If you disagree with some of the purposes, how could you change them?

7. What do you consider the three most important assumptions that would influence your teaching with an integrated curriculum (see section C. Assumptions for an Integrated Curriculum)? Explain.

Individual Notes

Chapter

2

Initiating an Interdisciplinary Thematic Unit

The most beautiful thing we can experience is the mysterious. It is the source of all true art and science.

—Albert Einstein

INTERDISCIPLINARY THEMATIC UNIT FOR ELEMENTARY SCHOOL STUDENTS: *KEEPERS OF THE EARTH*

In 1992, Mary Lee Hahn and Sherry Goubeux, primary-grade teachers, incorporated some exciting science activities into one of their thematic units, called Keepers of the Earth. To begin, they located various resources, including children's books related to different aspects of the main topic, the environment. They also found useful poetry and prose in books related to the subtopics of daily lesson plans, such as Learning from Our Mistakes, Action Plans for the Environment, Animals and Plants, Recycling, and Nature's Balance, Recovery, and Interconnections.

After sharing information about nature with the students, the teachers let the students take the lead in devising activities related to the environment. A few students proposed a fund raiser to raise money to buy trees to plant in the woods behind their school, an idea that developed into a used-toy sale at a regional "Country Fair." After some discussion, the students decided to create a bird sanctuary near the school, because nearby construction was encroaching on the wooded area. The money raised was designated for the purchase of several bird feeders as well as trees and shrubs that would attract the birds. The students advertised, gathered used toys, priced them, and worked at a booth at the fair. Another group of students showed an interest in plants, and these young "landscape architects," supported by their teachers, studied plant types and shopped for good prices.

The students prepared and presented the sanctuary proposal to the principal, the district director, and the head of the school grounds crew, as well as to representatives of Sherex Chemical Company, the school's community partner, which had offered to help fund the project. Once given the go-ahead, the students planted the newly purchased trees and shrubs for the bird sanctuary on a rainy day. Other classes helped mulch around the new plants. Interestingly, what had started as an idea of a few students in one class had turned into a project "owned" by the school and its community partner. Others in the school and community made contributions as well—second graders planted flowers, the parent-teacher organization purchased picnic tables for use as an outdoor classroom, and a local garden club donated bulbs.

● ●

K eepers of the Earth is an example of a well-done interdisciplinary unit, and its description may give you an idea of the power such a unit can have—the teacher initiates the unit in a way that develops in students an awareness and appreciation for a particular topic, and then they do something together that is positive, lasting, and important enough to get other people involved in various ways.

Chapter 1 introduced you to the purpose of an integrated curriculum and to the different levels of the spectrum of integrated curriculum. There was a brief discussion of the pros and cons of engaging students in today's diverse and multicultural classrooms with learning experiences through integrated curriculum and ITUs. Chapter 1 also emphasized theories that support the development and use of an integrated curriculum; the importance and value of using the community as a resource was reviewed.

In this chapter, you will be asked to suggest examples of ways to initiate units—perhaps one related to the environment, such as Hahn and Goubeux did in the chapter-opening vignette. The role of the teacher and the role of the student are considered. In one exercise, you are asked to select a theme for a unit, formulate questions to guide the study, and select resources related to those questions. In another exercise, you will collect information related to the scope and sequence of a unit in a classroom of your choice.

A.   Selecting a Theme for an Interdisciplinary Thematic Unit

When working within an integrated curriculum, students might study a theme on an ongoing basis. Themes that students suggest often relate to such ideas as friendship is important, fears can be overcome, self-understanding can be developed, and prejudice is a harmful force. Other themes might focus on the value of cooperation, of respecting authority, of accepting others, of getting support from others, of having a moral code to guide one's actions, and of establishing a positive relationship with an adult or a caring "other."

Some schools identify a theme for each grade, one that can be considered from the perspective of the past, the present, and the future and one that reflects the school's educational goals. An example is the theme of Self for first grade. Themes that have been commonly used for various grades include Self-Awareness, Human Behavior, Political and Citizenship Education, Economic Education, Environmental Education, Symbols of Freedom, and Heritage.

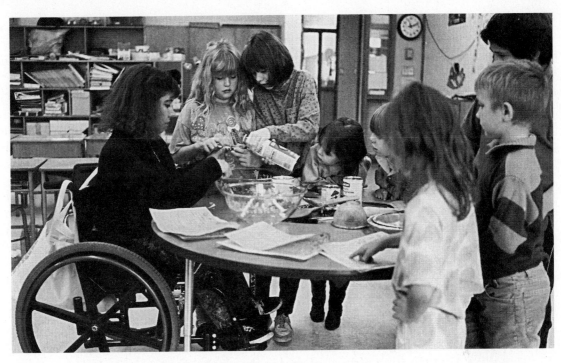

Students might study some themes on an ongoing basis, such as the value of cooperation. These students have found ways to work well together on an activity related to an ITU.

Sometimes, a teacher will identify a theme for a unit from school, district, or state documents. For instance, when natural science is the curriculum basis for a unit, a theme from a state's document might be Change and Continuity, Systems and Interactions, or Evolution and Energy. At other times, a teacher will refer to such planning documents as those published by the National Council for the Social Studies (NCSS) and other groups. Such documents are useful in developing interdisciplinary thematic units and determining their place in the scope and sequence of instructional programs (National Council for the Social Studies, 1990). This example from a recent NCSS document identifies various themes:

Kindergarten:	Awareness of Self in a Social Setting
First Grade:	The Individual in Primary Social Groups, i.e., Understanding School and Family Life
Second Grade:	Meeting Basic Needs in Nearby Social Groups, i.e., the Neighborhood
Third Grade:	Sharing Earth's Resources with Others, i.e., the Community
Fourth Grade:	Understanding Human Life in Varied Environments, i.e., the Region
Fifth Grade:	Understanding People of the Americas, i.e., the United States and Its Close Neighbors
Sixth Grade:	Understanding People and Cultures, i.e., the Eastern Hemisphere
Seventh Grade:	Understanding a Changing World of Many Nations, i.e., a Global View
Eighth Grade:	Building a Strong and Free Nation, i.e., the United States

Ninth Grade:	Understanding Systems That Make a Democratic Society Work, i.e., Law, Justice, and Economics
Tenth Grade:	Understanding Origins of Major Cultures, i.e., a World History
Eleventh Grade:	The Maturing of America, i.e., History of the United States
Twelfth Grade:	Selections usually made from: (1) Issues and Problems of Modern Society and (2) Introduction to the Social Sciences

At other times, the teacher might want to identify a theme that is more specifically related to a particular discipline, such as history. The following, based on the recommendations of the 1988 Bradley Commission on History in Schools, are examples related to history:

- Civilization, cultural diffusion, and innovation, i.e., the evolution of major civilizations;
- Human interaction with the environment, i.e., people's choices made available by geography;
- Values, beliefs, political ideas, and institutions, i.e., the evolution of democratic societies;
- Conflict and cooperation, causes of conflicts and war, and approaches to peace;
- Comparative history of major developments, i.e., revolutionary, reactionary, and reform periods across time and place; and
- Social and political interactions, i.e., changes in class, ethnic, gender, and racial relations and patterns.

After a theme is selected, teachers and students often develop guiding questions in order to help focus the interdisciplinary study. Here are some examples:

- How Did African Americans Begin Their Journey to Freedom?
- What Went on during Columbus's Journeys?
- Why Can Some Constructions Be Called Grand Constructions?
- What Are the Reasons People Celebrate Liberty? How Do They Celebrate?
- Who Are the Keepers of the Earth? What Do They Do?

B. The Process of Selecting a Theme

When selecting a theme, the process differs depending on whether the teacher is working independently or as part of a team. In this and subsequent sections of this chapter, that basic difference is taken into consideration as we walk you through the steps of selecting a theme for an ITU.

Working Independently

If you are working alone, you should first list all of the possible themes and topics that you can find in any existing course outlines. As you make this list, note any of the themes and topics that might relate to specific subject areas. Then decide on a theme or topic that can be correlated with each subject area without violating the educational plans for which you are responsible during the academic year. Sometimes you may have to select content from two or more units that you have planned previously; at other times you may want to integrate some content from previous units. If a theme for the ITU under consideration is not yet apparent, now is the time to select one, using the topic(s) you (perhaps with your students) have earmarked in your list. Critique your theme by examining it for various characteristics. The questions in Figure 2.1 should help you in this critique (see also Planning Master 4).

Working with Team Members

Often a team of teachers from specific areas of the curriculum in a middle school or high school will collaborate in teaching an interdisciplinary thematic unit. The first step in such cases is to discuss how the unit will proceed as a collective effort on the part of everyone. In other words, all of the team teachers—and other faculty, if desired—should be encouraged to participate as equally as possible.

Together, the team members must reach a consensus about what the students should gain from the interdisciplinary unit. For example, you might want to discuss some of the subject-specific frameworks, goals, objectives, curriculum guides, textbooks, supplemental materials, and units that are already available for the academic instruction. The discussion among team members should also focus on what each member will teach. That will help clarify the scope and sequence of the unit, so that all of the teachers have an understanding of what can and can't be done. Be realistic—talk about any limitations and constraints you see in this undertaking. Taking time to play the part of educational "troubleshooters" will enable the team to identify various stumbling blocks before they impede the progress of the unit, making implementation of the ITU go more smoothly. For example, members may want to clarify the purpose of working together, write a mission statement for the team, and make suggestions for turning that statement into a working plan.

An ITU pulls material from across the curriculum, and therefore the team will need to review the information that each of the team teachers presents from his or her subject area. Together, members should list all of the possible topics that can be found in any existing course outlines. Remember, dialogue is important and compromise is inevitable—a give and take is needed in these discussions because some themes or topics will correlate with certain subject areas better than with other areas. Also keep in mind that as team teachers the goal is to find a theme or topic that "works" for all members. You all will want a theme or topic that can be correlated with each subject

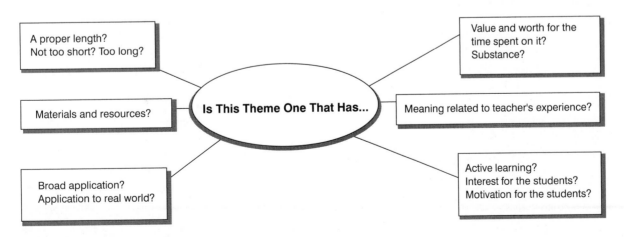

Figure 2.1   Critiquing a Theme

area without destroying the educational plans that all team teachers individually have for instruction during the academic year.

In some cases, the team may have to select content from units that one or more teachers have planned previously. In other cases, the team may have to merge some content from previous units. At this point, if a theme for the ITU has not yet become apparent, the time has come to derive a theme from the topic(s) team members have put forward. Once selected, a theme should be critiqued by examining it for various characteristics. The questions in Figure 2.1 may be of help in this critique.

To further gain insight into the process of selecting a theme for an ITU, turn your attention to Exercise 2.1, Beginning an ITU. Then continue your study by doing Exercise 2.2, Beginning an ITU: Investigating Specific Questions and Identifying Selected Resources, and Exercise 2.3, Beginning an ITU: Identifying Critical Thinking Processes.

EXERCISE 2.1
Beginning an ITU

• • • • • •

Instructions.   The purpose of this exercise is to work with a partner or partners to gain insight into selecting a theme for an ITU. First, divide your class into partnerships representing elementary, middle, or high school interests, and then have two or more partnerships work together. Each group is to decide the grade level for which their ITU will be suitable.

1. If desired, simulate a cooperative group structure, assigning the following roles to members in each group of partnerships (if this is not desired, move on to step 2):

   Facilitator. The one responsible for seeing that every member in the group gets the assistance that he or she needs.

   Checker. The one responsible for seeing that every member finishes his or her work for the day.

   Reporter. The one responsible for discussing what the group members learned during the ending debriefing session held each day after group work.

2. The first task is to select a theme for study, just as the students in your classroom could self-select their lines of inquiry.

   Theme:

   What sources will you consult *before* you finally select a theme?   *Yes*   *No*

   a. School, district, and state curriculum guides for your grade
      level   _____   _____

   b. Student textbooks and teacher's manual for state adopted
      textbooks   _____   _____

   c. Student interests and questions   _____   _____

   d. Professional literature related to education   _____   _____

   e. Other

3. Working individually, brainstorm as many word and phrase associations about the group theme as possible. Write the theme in the center of the space below and group your associations around the theme (i.e., construct a web). Then show your work to others in your group.

4. Join a small group or the total group and contribute the word and phrase associations from step 3 to the common sharing of ideas. Have a volunteer write everyone's ideas in the form of a graphic web, and then replicate the web in the space below. Take notes on any discussion about it. Keep the web for reference as you continue your study of ITUs.

5. Ask any questions you have related to any of the words and phrases on the web. Assist the group members as they classify all of the members' questions into categories. Draw lines to connect any related categories, and then label the categories with headings of your choice. Make a sketch of the categories and their labels in the space that follows:

EXERCISE 2.2

Beginning an ITU: Investigating Specific Questions and Identifying Selected Resources

• • • • • •

Instructions.   The purpose of this exercise is to develop you skills in investigating specific questions and in selecting resources related to an interdisciplinary thematic unit. For this exercise, use the theme and questions your group developed in Exercise 2.1.

1. From Exercise 2.1, select three (or more) questions about the group's theme that you would like to investigate.

   a.

   b.

   c.

   Other:

2. Now focus on the interdisciplinary aspect of the unit by writing questions about the theme from the perspective of people from various disciplines. You might begin with the disciplines that are closely related to your theme. Ask yourself, "What would an anthropologist want to know about this theme? an artist? a biologist? an historian? a mathematician? a sociologist?" Writing these questions will help you determine how many subject areas you will incorporate in your thematic unit—a great many or just a few? Consult with others in your class if necessary. For each of the disciplines, an example is given related to an ITU you will examine in chapter 5, called Early Explorers and Settlers in North America. Use the examples to spur your own thinking.

   Anthropologist [*Example*: How have anthropologists helped us learn about the topic? How can we discover a relationship about the people's behavior and their beliefs?]

Artist [*Example*: How can we show what we know about the topic through art, music, dance, etc.? What contributions did art, music, and dance make in the lives of early explorers and settlers?]

Historian [*Example*: What contributions did history make in the lives of explorers and early settlers? How have historicans helped us learn about the topic? How has the acceptance or rejection of the idea of colonies changed through time?]

Mathematician [*Example*: In what ways did early explorers and settlers use mathematics? In what ways can we express what we know about the topic through mathematics? How have mathematicians helped us learn about this topic?]

Sociologist [*Example*: What groups in society operate to bring us information about the topic? How have sociologists contributed to the topic?]

Other:

3. Reread your questions and underline words that represent concepts to be learned. What generalizations (big ideas) related to the theme can be written related to this thematic study?

4. Select one or more of your generalizations. Then look at the student textbooks, the teachers' manuals, and the curriculum guidelines for your grade to see if your generalizations can be taught through a topic identified in any of these resources. What did you discover?

5. For each question that you selected for further study (step 1), identify the resources you could or would consult to investigate the question further. Resources can range from using the community as a laboratory to reading printed material. Make a list of the resources.

EXERCISE 2.3

Beginning an ITU: Identifying Critical Thinking Processes

• • • • • •

Instructions.   The purpose of this exercise is to develop your skills in identifying the critical thinking you used in Exercises 2.1 and 2.2. In this exercise, you will review the steps you did in the previous two exercises and reflect upon the critical thinking that each step required of you.

     The specific intellectual processes used in this exercise were derived from Benjamin S. Bloom's *Taxonomy of Educational Objectives, Book I: Cognitive Domain* (1984). Bloom's taxonomy arranges intellectual processes from the simplest to the most complex in six categories—knowledge, comprehension, application, analysis, synthesis, and evaluation.

1. By referring to the steps in the previous exercises, think of an example of how you used each of the intellectual processes listed below. For each of your examples, briefly describe the way in which you engaged in that type of critical thinking.

   Knowledge (listing, naming, telling, defining, recording, labeling, collecting, specifying, enumerating). When did you recognize and recall information?

   Comprehension (recognizing, locating, retelling, identifying, restating, describing, explaining, reporting, translating, summarizing). When did you understand the meaning of the information you received?

   Application (showing, illustrating, practicing, exhibiting, demonstrating, dramatizing, simulating, calculating, applying). When did you use any of the information you received?

Analysis (comparing, contrasting, arranging, organizing, diagramming, grouping, questioning, interpreting, inquiring). When did you use your ability to dissect information into component parts and see relationships?

Synthesis (assembling, constructing, creating, inventing, predicting, producing, developing, originating, hypothesizing, incorporating). When did you put components together to form a new idea?

Evaluation (measuring, estimating, criticizing, recommending, judging, revising, choosing). When did you judge the worth of an idea, notion, theory, thesis, proposition, or opinion?

2. Your purpose in the first three exercises of this chapter has been to gain insight into an interdisciplinary thematic unit of study. Now that you have completed the exercises, what insight(s) about starting an interdisciplinary thematic unit of study have you gained? Discuss this with others.

C. Identifying the Unit by Name

Whether you are working alone or with others, you are now at a point where the ITU represents a topic and has a theme that you have assigned to it. Now is the time to give the unit a name. Discuss with students ways the ITU is meaningful to the members of the class and the school and integrated to real-life experiences, and thus important. You will want to emphasize that the major part of the value of the unit will come from its interdisciplinary approach.

D. Developing Scope and Sequence for Content and Instruction

Working Independently

Once the theme has been selected and a name given to the unit, the time has come to assign dates to certain topics in the unit and to identify activities in a logical sequence. This sequence could incorporate any or a combination of the following arrangements:

1. A primary focus on a single content area. For example, history/social studies plays the most important role in the unit's sequence of activities, though a multitude of other areas may be included in the activities as well. Consider an ITU whose theme is Children and Their Families in America's Colonies, with a primary focus on history/social studies. The sequence of activities might include several related to history/social studies, such as the colonists' connections to the rest of the world, their activities in their daily lives, their economic status, and their beliefs and manners. Each of the activities, or study areas, could comprise a certain time period—perhaps a week or a month. During each period, students would learn within an historical context as they explore art, biographies of famous people, drama, music, and literature, as well as how the politics of the time affected children and their families.
2. An equal focus on two content areas. For example, both history/social studies and English/Language Arts play equal roles of importance in the unit's sequence of activities. A teacher might draw upon children's literature to establish connections

Working independently, this teacher takes the time to plan the activities of the unit in a logical sequence.

in order to make the time period and the theme Children and Their Families in America's Colonies come alive for the students. In this arrangement, there is an emphasis on English literature to provide the background needed to bring the lives of the people of the time to the attention of the students.

3. An equal focus on three (or more) content areas. For example history/social studies, English/Language Arts, and science play equal roles of importance in the unit's sequence of activities. The teacher's goal is to integrate the areas just as they are integrated in our real lives. For a unit whose theme is Children and Their Families in America's Colonies, the teacher can engage the students not only in the activities mentioned in the first two arrangements but also in science activities. The teacher might assist the students in locating the colony of Jamestown on a map, or ask them to research climatic conditions at the time and what wildlife was prevalent in that region.

You may find it valuable to give a copy of the sequence of your activities to a teaching colleague. Ask for your colleague's suggestions about the activities and the sequence you have identified. If most of the remarks are positive, you will know that the sequence you planned appears workable from another's point of view. If there are difficulties, you may want to consider modifications in the activities themselves or in the sequence in which they are offered.

In planning and selecting learning activities, it is important to select activities that are as direct as possible. You will want to have your students involved in direct hands-on experiences to encourage the full use of their learning modalities—auditory, visual, tactile, and kinesthetic—which will lead to the most effective and long-lasting learning. Figure 2.2 classifies examples of learning experiences. Notice that the most concrete experiences—Direct Experiences—are the most engaging for the learner.

Working with Team Members

During a common planning time, team members must work together to schedule dates, coordinate topics, and identify activities in a logical sequence. Members might take turns being the team leader in order to facilitate the flow of ideas and also address openly and realistically any anxieties produced during unit planning. Sometimes, taking an "anxiety break" for a few minutes allows members to regain the composure necessary for arriving at a group decision that will best promote the students' learning.

E.   Providing Time Lines

Working Independently

With the school calendar in mind, you must make a time line, or schedule, for the ITU that is suitable for you and your students. Write down important dates, including dates that you will need to have certain material prepared and the beginning and closing dates of the unit study. Indicate dates that will be important to the students, such as when reports are due and when the final culminating activity will be held.

Working with Team Members

A team must also make a detailed time line, one that is suitable for all members of the teaching team. This time line, called Time Line A, should contain a record of all dates

Verbal Experiences

Teacher talk, written words: engaging one sense: using the most abstract symbolization: students are physically inactive.

Example 1: Listening to the teacher talk about tide pools.

Example 2: Listening to a student report about the Grand Canyon in Arizona.

Example 3: Listening to a guest speaker talk about the state legislature while showing slides of it in action.

Visual Experiences

Still pictures, diagrams, charts: engaging one sense; typically symbolic; students are physically inactive.

Example 1: Viewing slide photographs of tide pools.

Example 2: Viewing drawings and photographs of the Grand Canyon.

Example 3: Listening to a guest speaker talk about the state legislature whil showing slides of it in action.

Vicarious Experiences

Laser videodisc programs; computer programs: video programs: engaging more than one sense; learner is indirectly "doing"; may be some limited physical activity.

Example 1: Interacting with a computer program about wave action and life in tide pools.

Example 2: Viewing and listening to a video program about the Grand Canyon.

Example 3: Taking a field trip to observe the state legislature in action.

Simulated Experiences

Role playing; experimenting; simulations; mock-up; working models; all or nearly all senses are engaged; activity often integrates disciplines; closest to the real thing.

Example 1: Building a classroom working model of a tide pool.

Example 2: Building a classroom working model of the Grand Canyon.

Example 3: Designing a classroom role-play simulation patterned after the operating procedure of the state legislature.

Direct Experiences

Learner is actually doing what is being learned; true inquiry; all senses are engaged; usually integrates disciplines; the real thing.

Example 1: Visiting and experiencing a tide pool.

Example 2: Visiting and experiencing the Grand Canyon.

Example 3: Designing an elected representative body to oversee the operation of the school within-the-school program, one that is patterned after the state legislative assembly.

Figure 2.2   The Learning Experiences Ladder

by which any assigned work must be done by a team member—that is, any work that must be completed for the development of the ITU. The team should then turn its attention to a second time line, Time Line B, which should contain all dates important to the students as well as to the teachers. For example, Time Line B should indicate when the ITU begins (and in which periods), various due dates during the unit, and when the ITU ends.

Now explore the scope and sequence of an ITU by doing Exercise 2.4, Making Some Decisions Early: More about Scope and Sequence, and Exercise 2.5, Developing the Scope and Sequence of Initial Weekly Plans for an ITU.

EXERCISE 2.4

Making Some Decisions Early: More about Scope and Sequence

• • • • • •

Instructions.   The purpose of this exercise is to begin planning the scope and sequence of your interdisciplinary thematic unit. In your ITU plan, you want to incorporate the major concepts and generalizations that are in the curriculum guide for your grade level, as well as the ones you identified in Exercise 2.2. You also need to make various decisions about grouping, unit length, unit structure, and disciplines to be included.

1. *Individual Work and Group Work.* You might plan to have all types of grouping in your thematic unit. For example, you could begin each day or period with a theme and then have students work with partners or in small groups. As an alternative, you could invite students to participate in a whole-group study of the theme and then ask students to request—and thus "reserve"—one area of study for individual inquiry. Decisions you want to make about individual work and group work:

2. *Length of Study.* Your unit can be of varying lengths. You might develop an ITU for a two-week grading period or a six-week grading period. You might plan four separate ITUs during the entire year, or you might plan another length of your choice. Decisions about length of study:

3. *Concentrated Structure and Expanded Structure.* You might decide on an expanded structure, where the students have common experiences in a whole group situation, and then have students select separate areas of study to explore as individual or small-groups inquiries. On the other hand, you could decide on a concentrated structure, where the students learn mainly in whole-group situations with some partnership and small-group work. With a concentrated structure, the students realize the ITU has a beginning and an end. Decisions about structure:

4. *Disciplines to Include.* You might decide to include a great many subject areas or just a few. Decisions about disciplines:

EXERCISE 2.5

Developing the Scope and Sequence of Initial Weekly Plans for an ITU

• • • • • •

Instructions.   The purpose of this exercise is to develop the scope and sequence of an interdisciplinary thematic unit of study. For the purposes of this exercise, assume that you are interested in planning a three-week unit. Work with a partner or small group as you plan.

1. Select one of your generalizations related to your theme (Exercise 2.2, step 3) and write it in the appropriate space that follows. Review the students' texts to determine the extent of any material related to the thematic study. Write the page numbers or chapter numbers from the texts for future reference. If different generalizations are to be the foci of the other remaining weeks, review the texts for the material related to those generalizations, too.

Theme:

First Week

Generalization/overall question to focus on (underline words that reflect concepts):

	Science	*Social Sciences*	*Expressive Arts*	*Math*
Pages/chapters				

Ways teacher gives input:

Ways students give input:

Second Week
Generalization/overall guiding question to focus on (underline words that reflect concepts):

	Science	*Social Sciences*	*Expressive Arts*	*Math*
Pages/chapters				

Ways teacher gives input:

Ways students give input:

Third Week
Generalization/overall guiding question to focus on (underline words that reflect concepts):

	Science	*Social Sciences*	*Expressive Arts*	*Math*
Pages/chapters				

Ways teacher gives input:

Ways students give input:

2. If your ITU is planned for longer than three weeks, develop further initial weekly plans in a format similar to the first three.

3. What plans do you have for your students to take an active part in the development of the thematic unit? (*Examples*: developing a question map; reserving a particular question for individual inquiry; suggesting resources and references to search for information; naming community resources; hands-on activities; small group work; whole group instructional conversations)

F.   Relying on the Community as a Resource

People

The people of the community—especially parents and other relatives of the students—can make a significant contribution to the thematic unit. When invited with care, a community-resource person can be asked to spend time with the students for an instructional purpose related to the unit. A quick survey of the yellow pages in your telephone directory can provide a wealth of information about the people who could serve as resources. For example, a member of the local historical society could bring photographs of early life in the community and speak to the students from the point of view of someone interested in history.

The students should always be prepared for the visitor. They should write down any questions they would like to ask in an informal interview. And students must be prepared to demonstrate the courtesies that are extended to guests. After the visit, the students can write thank-you letters to the guest—perhaps mentioning what impressed them, some of the things they learned, ways the guest changed their thoughts, and what they thought about after the visit. Resource people who might be invited as visitors/interviewees include:

athlete	attorney	author
artist	bank teller	businessperson
city official	clergy	community worker
dentist	environmentalist	exchange student
historian	judge	landscaper
legislator	medical doctor	meteorologist
military rep	news anchor	nurse
paramedic	pilot	professor
reporter	salesperson	

Places

When you want to have students visit a place off the school campus, you must think through the details of the trip so you can plan ways to make it relate to the ITU and so you can anticipate any problem that might arise during the outing. For all trips, you will want to have a purpose, keep the safety of the students foremost in mind, and create good public relations between the students and the citizens in the community.

Student Choices. A class meeting is often helpful to help focus the students' attention on decisions to be made about a field trip—should you choose to discuss a possible trip and elicit input from the students. Figure 2.3 shows a sample web that can be used as a discussion focus, suitable for an overhead transparency (Planning Master 5). With this web as a model, the students can write their own headings, questions, responses, and responsibilities on a blank transparency.

In your community, there will be many places that teacher and students can visit. The teacher should select those that will contribute to the students' understanding of the study—related geography, history, and current events. Some of the places that can make an educational contribution to an ITU are shown in Figure 2.4.

Enrichment and Extracurricular Activities

To build more involvement between the students and the community, as well as to help students in their career goals, the teacher can introduce some of the students to various

Purpose: *To prepare a field guide for other students who will be traveling to the site.*

Written permission needed:

What do we want to know?

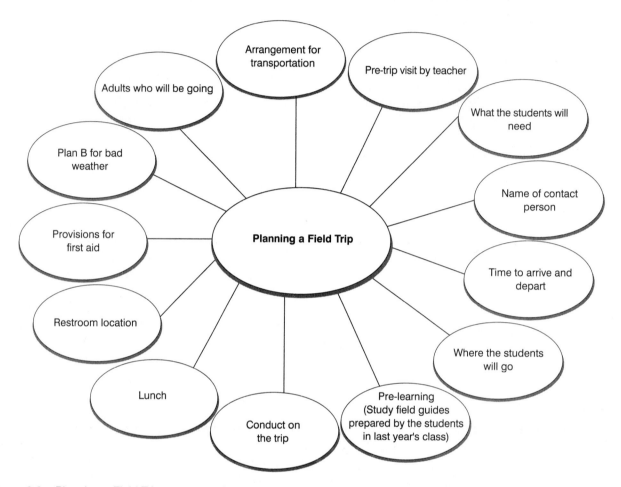

Figure 2.3   Planning a Field Trip

enrichment and extracurricular activities. For example, a teacher might introduce students to the school district's annual science fair and to the state's achievement programs in mathematics, engineering and science, which usually are of interest to the students who are looking at future technical careers. Perhaps various community action groups in the area offer after-school programs and clubs that the students need to know about. In addition, the teacher can search for various incentive programs affiliated with regional colleges or universities that are dedicated to students' selected career goals.

G.   Sharing Materials

Working Independently

When working independently, you may find it of value to give a copy of your unit to a trusted colleague you consider a friend. Ask that colleague for comments and sugges-

airports and bus terminals	assembly factories
aquariums	art galleries
bakeries and canneries	broadcasting stations
canals, creeks, delta ways, docks, tributaries	courthouse
factories and warehouses	fish hatcheries
fire stations and earthquake center offices	flood plains, wetlands, and rivers
farms and ranches	government bodies in session
historical monuments and sites	hospitals
health care agencies	harbors
libraries	museums
newspapers	police stations
parks and nature areas	post offices
railroad and light rail stations	refineries
telephone companies	transportation offices
science centers	shopping areas
weather bureaus	zoos

Figure 2.4 Resource Places in the Community

tions about the unit, including any suggestions about print and nonprint materials. Your unit cannot function without materials, and so you must plan for the resources that are needed, including audiovisual equipment, references, reading materials, and community resources.

If most of your colleague's remarks are positive, you will know that the unit you planned appears workable from another's point of view. If there are difficulties, you may want to consider more modifications in the ITU.

Working with Team Members

When working with a team, you will find it necessary for each member to provide other team members with two copies of his or her draft unit. Each member then reviews the draft copies of other members, particularly examining a member's attention to the organization of the materials—audiovisual materials, reference books, reading sources, resource people, and other community resources. Each member then returns one of the two copies to each of the other members, with comments and suggestions, keeping the other copy in order to plan complementary lessons. Depending on the comments and suggestions from other team members, a member can have confidence in his or her plan or make modifications as needed.

Summary

In this chapter, we gave an overview of one way to initiate an ITU, including selecting a theme to study, formulating an overall guiding question or questions for the unit, and planning the scope and sequence of the unit. We suggested that you use guiding questions to isolate concept words and then use the concept words to write generalizations that represent knowledge related to the thematic study. As in the previous chapter, we want to reiterate that our suggestions in this guide are guidelines—not universals and absolutes for developing an ITU.

Questions and Activities for Discussion

1. The use of community resources can add a great deal to your students' background knowledge and frame of reference for learning. What suggestions for community involvement in an ITU do you have?

2. How would you plan an interdisciplinary lesson of an ITU for a classroom of diverse students? In small groups, plan a single lesson for a classroom of multicultural students. Decide on the grade level and the diversity of the students. You might begin by brainstorming ideas about aspects of the lesson and then arrange the appropriate aspects into a sequence for the lesson. Identify the hands-on activities and learning resources you would want to use—the audiovisual materials, books, computer programs, music, realia, and community resources.

Individual Notes

Chapter

· ·

3

Developing Objectives and Learning Activities

· ·

I think and think for months and years. Ninety-nine times the conclusion is false. The hundredth time I am right.

—*Albert Einstein*

· ·

INTERDISCIPLINARY THEMATIC UNIT: *THE DINOSAURS*

Much recent educational research has focused on teachers who have been consistently identified as "effective." In discussing the findings of studies related to the skills of such effective teachers, Garcia (1994) points out that one characteristic of those teachers is that they worked from a thematic curriculum as much as possible. In most cases once a theme was determined, usually in consultation with the students, the teachers planned instruction around a series of activities that focused on that theme. Examples of themes are the use of pesticides in the agricultural fields, the source of the local water supply, and the dinosaurs of prehistory.

The unit on dinosaurs encompassed a number of activities related to the theme, but each was also related to a different discipline:

- *History.* The students visited a museum that featured dinosaur exhibits.
- *Mathematics.* The students categorized types and graphed different sizes of dinosaurs.
- *Reading and Writing.* The students wrote stories about a favorite dinosaur.
- *Science.* The students speculated on the events that led to the dinosaurs' disappearance.

In the Elk Grove Unified School District in Elk Grove, California, Kristie Darras, a second-grade teacher, guided her students in a study of dinosaurs. The classroom activities integrated science and math, drawing and crafts, and music and reading, publishing original books to support the study. Connecting reading to music, the students listened to a song about each dinosaur being studied. Students read sentence strips with the words of the song. They added sound effects, sang the song several times, and added a rhythmic beat with their fingers and hands. Additionally, the students prepared their own dinosaur-shape books, wrote original pages, and created illustrations. To survey favorite dinosaurs, graphing was introduced. The students built their own graph in the classroom by drawing a favorite dinosaur and contributing it to a large graph. The students used individual copies of the graph to record what was added to the large graph and marked **X**'s with their pencils in the appropriate places. When the class graph was finished, the students read it with the teacher's guidance and talked about the information they had gathered.

The unit was culminated at the school's Open House night. Each student's homework for Open House was to bring an adult and to tell that person what he or she was learning at school. That night, the students told their visitors about dinosaurs and showed the dinosaur books, dinosaur mobiles, dinosaur body shapes made from felt, and dinosaur clay models they had made.[1]

• •

This guide was developed specifically to assist you in designing a unit for an integrated curriculum. In developing an ITU, you need to write an overview of the scope and sequence of the thematic study, as you did in Chapter 2, but you also need to plan the specific learning activities that will be the heart of the unit. As we pointed out in Chapter 2, the teacher can use the questions generated by the theme as foci and then locate resources that might be useful in exploring those questions. Information from such resources can be recorded by the students in various ways—in charts, graphs, notes in learning logs, and so on.

In this chapter we discuss how to develop the objectives and learning activities for an ITU. In exercises, you will be asked to initiate an ITU with a question map and then plan other learning activities—including a culminating activity—that will be suitable for your students. In one exercise, you take the role of a student who participates in personal inquiry (as you will ask your own students to do); you will be asked to select one question as an overall guiding question and then collect information related to that question from various resources.

In a subsequent exercise, you will be asked to reflect on your personal inquiry. The chapter ends with a number of exercises through which you write a teaching plan that includes objectives, resources, and learning activities.

A. Writing Behavioral Objectives

As with any instructional unit, the teacher (or team) must write behavioral objectives for the interdisciplinary thematic unit being planned. When writing behavioral objectives, you must ask yourself, How is the student to demonstrate that the objective has been reached? The objective must include an *action* that demonstrates that the objective has been achieved. This portion of the objective is sometimes referred to as the *terminal behavior* and sometimes as the *anticipated measurable performance*.

The ABCDs of Writing Objectives

When completely written, a behavioral objective has four components. To aid in your understanding, you might remember this as the ABCDs of writing behavioral objectives.

A.   The first of these components is the *Audience*—that is, the student(s) for whom the objective is intended. To address this component, teachers sometimes begin their objectives with the phrase "The student will be able to . . . " or, to personalize the objective, "You will be able to. . . . "

B.   The second component of a behavioral objective is the expected student *Behavior*. This expected performance must be written with action verbs, or verbs that call for measurable behavior. The reason for using action verbs is that only through directly observable, or measurable, behavior can the teacher assess whether the objective has been reached. Some verbs indicate behavior that is too vague (covert behavior) or too ambiguous or clearly not measurable.

When writing behavioral objectives, you should avoid verbs that clearly represent behaviors that are not directly observable, such as *appreciate, believe, comprehend, enjoy, know, learn, like,* and *understand*. Figure 3.1 lists verbs that you should consider using when writing behaviorable objectives. Those verbs do call for measurable behaviors.

C.   The third component of a behavioral objective is the *Conditions*—the setting in which the behavior will be demonstrated by the student and observed by the teacher. Consider this objective: "Each student will correctly identify ten different musical instruments by listening to a tape recording of the Boston Pops Symphony Orchestra and orally tell the class which instrument is being played at different times, as specified by the teacher." For students to be able to "correctly identify ten different musical instruments," the conditions are: "by listening to a tape recording of the Boston Pops Symphony Orchestra." And for "orally tell . . . which instrument is playing," the conditions are: "different times, as specified by the teacher."

D.   The fourth component of a behavioral objective—though not always included in objectives written by teachers—is the *Degree* or the level of expected performance. This is the component that allows for the assessment of student learning. When mastery learning is expected (achievement of 85 to 100 percent), the level of expected performance is usually omitted from the written objective (because it is understood).

Performance level is used to evaluate student achievement, and sometimes it is used to evaluate the effectiveness of the teaching. Student grades might be based on performance levels; the evaluation of teacher effectiveness might be based on the level of student performance.

B.   Classifying Behavioral Objectives

When planning instructional objectives, you should consider the three domains of learning objectives:

- *Cognitive*. This domain involves mental operations from the lowest level of the simple recall to complex, high-level evaluative processes.

1. Creative Behaviors

Alter	Generalize	Question	Regroup	Rephrase	Rewrite
Ask	Modify	Rearrange	Rename	Restate	Simplify
Change	Paraphrase	Recombine	Reorder	Restructure	Synthesize
Design	Predict	Reconstruct	Reorganize	Retell	Systematize

2. Complex, Logical, Judgmental Behaviors

Analyze	Combine	Contrast	Designate	Formulate	Plan
Appraise	Compare	Criticize	Determine	Generate	Structure
Assess	Conclude	Deduce	Discover	Induce	Substitute
		Defend	Evaluate	Infer	Suggest

3. General Discriminative Behaviors

Choose	Describe	Discriminate	Indicate	Match	Place
Collect	Detect	Distinguish	Isolate	Omit	Point
Define	Differentiate	Identify	List	Order	Select
				Pick	Separate

4. Social Behaviors

Accept	Answer	Cooperate	Forgive	Laugh	Reply
Admit	Argue	Dance	Greet	Meet	Smile
Agree	Communicate	Disagree	Help	Participate	Talk
Aid	Compliment	Discuss	Interact	Permit	Thank
Allow	Contribute	Excuse	Invite	Praise	Visit
			Join	React	Volunteer

5. Language Behaviors

Abbreviate	Call	Indent	Punctuate	Speak	Tell
Accent	Capitalize	Outline	Read	Spell	Translate
Alphabetize	Edit	Print	Recite	State	Verbalize
Articulate	Hyphenate	Pronounce	Say	Summarize	Whisper
			Sign	Syllabicate	Write

6. Study Behaviors

Arrange	Cite	Diagram	Itemize	Mark	Record
Categorize	Classify	Find	Label	Name	Reproduce
Chart	Compile	Follow	Locate	Note	Search
Circle	Copy	Gather	Look	Organize	Sort
			Map	Quote	Underline

7. Music Behaviors

Blow	Clap	Finger	Hum	Pluck	Strum
Bow	Compose	Harmonize	Mute	Practice	Tap
			Play	Sing	Whistle

8. Physical Behaviors

Arch	Climb	Hit	March	Ski	Swim
Bat	Face	Hop	Pitch	Skip	Swing
Bend	Float	Jump	Pull	Somersault	Throw
Carry	Grab	Kick	Push	Stand	Toss
Catch	Grasp	Knock	Run	Step	Walk
Chase	Grip	Lift	Skate	Stretch	

Figure 3.1   Verbs for Use in Stating Specific Learning Objectives

9. Arts Behaviors

Assemble	Cut	Frame	Mold	Roll	Stamp
Blend	Dab	Hammer	Nail	Rub	Stick
Brush	Dot	Handle	Paint	Saw	Stir
Build	Draw	Heat	Paste	Sculpt	Trace
Carve	Drill	Illustrate	Pat	Send	Trim
Color	Fold	Melt	Polish	Shake	Varnish
Construct	Form	Mix	Pour	Sketch	Wipe
			Press	Smooth	Wrap

10. Drama Behaviors

Act	Direct	Enter	Imitate	Pantomime	Respond
Clasp	Display	Exit	Leave	Pass	Show
Cross	Emit	Express	Move	Perform	Sit
				Proceed	Turn

11. Mathematical Behaviors

Add	Compute	Estimate	Integrate	Plot	Subtract
Bisect	Count	Extract	Interpolate	Prove	Sum
Calculate	Cumulate	Extrapolate	Measure	Reduce	Tabulate
Check	Derive	Graph	Multiply	Solve	Tally
Circumscribe	Divide	Group	Number	Square	Verify

12. Laboratory Science Behaviors

Align	Conduct	Dissect	Keep	Plant	Set
Apply	Connect	Feed	Lengthen	Prepare	Specify
Attach	Convert	Grow	Limit	Remove	Straighten
Balance	Decrease	Increase	Manipulate	Replace	Time
Calibrate	Demonstrate	Insert	Operate	Report	Transfer
				Reset	Weigh

13. General Appearance, Health, and Safety Behaviors

Button	Comb	Eat	Fill	Taste	Unzip
Clean	Cover	Eliminate	Go	Tie	Wait
Clear	Dress	Empty	Lace	Unbutton	Wash
Close	Drink	Fasten	Stack	Uncover	Wear
			Stop	Untie	Zip

14. Miscellaneous

Aim	Erase	Hunt	Peel	Scratch	Store
Attempt	Expand	Include	Pin	Send	Strike
Attend	Extend	Inform	Position	Serve	Supply
Begin	Feel	Kneel	Present	Sew	Support
Bring	Finish	Lay	Produce	Share	Switch
Buy	Fit	Lead	Propose	Sharpen	Take
Come	Fix	Lend	Provide	Shoot	Tear
Complete	Flip	Let	Put	Shorten	Touch
Correct	Get	Light	Raise	Shovel	Try
Crease	Give	Make	Relate	Shut	Twist
Crush	Grind	Mend	Repair	Signify	Type
Develop	Guide	Miss	Repeat	Slide	Use
Distribute	Hand	Offer	Return	Slip	Vote
Do	Hang	Open	Ride	Spread	Watch
Drop	Hold	Pack	Rip	Stake	Weave
End	Hook	Pay	Save	Start	Work

Figure 3.1   *continued*

- *Affective*. This domain involves feelings, attitudes, and values, ranging from the lower levels of acquisition to the highest level of internalization and action.
- *Psychomotor*. This domain involves locomotor skills, from the simple manipulation of materials to the communication of ideas and, finally, to the highest level of creative performance.

Schools attempt to design learning experiences to meet the five areas of developmental needs of the total child: (1) intellectual, (2) physical, (3) psychological, (4) social, and (5) moral and ethical. As a teacher, you will want to include learning objectives that address each of these needs. The intellectual needs fall primarily within the cognitive domain, and the physical needs fall primarily within the psychomotor domain. The other needs fall mostly within the affective domain.

Too frequently, teachers focus on the cognitive domain, assuming that the psychomotor and affective domains will take care of themselves. Effective teachers, however, plan their teaching so that students are guided from the lowest to highest levels of operation within each of the three domains.

Three developmental hierarchies are discussed in the following sections in order to help you understand each of the five areas of needs. Notice the verbs listed for each level of a hierarchy. These verbs should help you fashion your behavioral objectives for the ITU lesson plans you will soon be developing.

Cognitive Domain Hierarchy

In a widely accepted taxonomy (classification) of objectives, Bloom and his associates classified cognitive objectives according to the complexity of the skills and abilities they embodied (Bloom et al., 1984). The result was a series of levels, hierarchy, ranging from the simplest to the most complex intellectual processes.

Prerequisite to a student's ability to function at one level of the hierarchy is the ability to function at the preceding level or levels. In other words, when a student is functioning at the third level of the cognitive domain, the student is automatically functioning at the first and second levels. (This concept holds true for the levels of the affective and psychomotor domains as well.)

The six major levels (or categories) in Bloom's taxonomy of cognitive objectives are:

1. *Knowledge*. Recognizing and recalling information.
2. *Comprehension*. Understanding the meaning of information.
3. *Application*. Using information.
4. *Analysis*. Dissecting information into its component parts to see their relationships.
5. *Synthesis*. Putting components together to form new ideas.
6. *Evaluation*. Judging the worth of an idea, notion, theory, thesis, proposition, information, or opinion.

Although space does not allow elaboration here, Bloom's taxonomy includes various sublevels within each of these six major levels. In our opinion, it is less important that you can classify an objective absolutely than it is that you can understand and recognize levels of thinking and doing. Also important is that you recognize the importance of attending to each student's intellectual behavior, from the lowest to the highest levels of operation in all three domains.[2] A discussion of each of Bloom's six categories follows.

Knowledge.   The basic element in Bloom's taxonomy concerns the acquisition of knowledge—that is, the ability to recognize and recall information. Although this is the lowest of the six levels, the information to be learned may not itself be of a low level. In fact, the information may be of an extremely high level. Bloom includes at this level knowledge of principles, generalizations, theories, structures, and methodologies, as well as facts and ways of dealing with facts.

Action verbs appropriate for this level include *choose, complete, define, describe, identify, indicate, list, locate, match, name, outline, recall, recognize, select,* and *state.* (Note that some verbs may be appropriately used at more than one cognitive level.)

These are examples of objectives at this level (note especially the verb used in each example):

- From memory, the student will recall the letters in the alphabet that are vowels.
- The student will list the organelles found in animal cell cytoplasm.
- The student will identify the major parts of speech in the sentence.
- The student will name the positions of players on a soccer team.

The remaining five levels of Bloom's taxonomy deal with the use of knowledge. They encompass the educational objectives aimed at developing cognitive skills and abilities, including comprehension, application, analysis, synthesis, and evaluation of knowledge.

Comprehension.   Comprehension includes the ability to translate, explain, or interpret knowledge, and to extrapolate from that knowledge to address new situations. Action verbs appropriate for this level include *change, classify, convert, defend, describe, estimate, expand, explain, generalize, infer, interpret, paraphrase, predict, summarize,* and *translate.*

These are examples of objectives at this level:

- Within a sentence, the student will recognize the letters that are vowels.
- The student will describe each of the organelles found in animal cell cytoplasm.
- The student will explain the major parts of speech in the sentence.
- The student will describe the positions of players on a soccer team.

Application.   Once students comprehend information, they should be able to apply it. Action verbs for this level include *apply, compute, demonstrate, develop, discover, modify, operate, participate, perform, plan, predict, relate, show,* and *use.*

These are examples of objectives at this level:

- The student will use in a sentence a word that contains at least two vowels.
- The student will relate the difference among the organelles found in animal cell cytoplasm in a reporting format of his/her choice.
- The student will demonstrate in a complete sentence each of the major parts of speech.
- The student will relate how the positions of players on a soccer team depend upon each other.

Analysis.   This level includes objectives that require students to use the skills of analysis. Action verbs appropriate for this level include *analyze, break down, categorize, classify, compare, contrast, debate, deduce, diagram, differentiate, discriminate, identify, illustrate, infer, outline, relate, separate,* and *subdivide.*

These are examples of objectives at this level:

- Given a list of words, the student will be able to differentiate those that contain one vowel from those that contain several.
- Using a microscope, the student will compare and contrast the organelles found in animal cell cytoplasm.
- The student will analyze a paragraph for misuse of major parts of speech.
- The student will illustrate, on the writing board or an overhead transparency, the different positions of players on a soccer team.

Synthesis. This level includes objectives that involve such skills as designing a plan, proposing a set of operations, and deriving a series of abstract relations. Action verbs appropriate for this level include *arrange, categorize, combine, compile, constitute, create, design, develop, devise, document, explain, formulate, generate, modify, organize, originate, plan, produce, rearrange, reconstruct, revise, rewrite, summarize, synthesize, tell, transmit,* and *write.*

These are examples of objectives at this level:

- Given a list of words, the student will be able to rearrange them into several lists according to the vowels contained in each.
- The student will devise a classification scheme for the organelles found in animal cell cytoplasm according to their functions.
- The student will write a paragraph that correctly uses each of the major arts of speech.
- The student will design, on the writing board or an overhead transparency, an offensive plan that uses the different positions of players on a soccer team.

Evaluation. This, the highest level of Bloom's taxonomy, includes offering opinions and making value judgments. Action verbs appropriate for this category include *appraise, argue, assess, compare, conclude, consider, contrast, criticize, decide, discriminate, evaluate, explain, interpret, judge, justify, rank, rate, relate, standardize, support,* and *validate.*

These are examples of objectives at this level:

- The student will evaluate other students' identifications of vowels in sentences written on the board.
- While observing living animal cell cytoplasm under the microscope, the student will justify his or her interpretation that certain structures are specific organelles.
- The student will assess a paragraph written by another student for the proper use of major parts of speech.
- The student will interpret the reasons for an opposing team's offensive use of the different positions of players on a soccer team.

Now, with Exercise 3.1, try to identify the level of objectives within the cognitive domain.

EXERCISE 3.1

Classifying Cognitive Objectives—A Self-check Exercise

• • • • • •

Instructions.   The purpose of this exercise is to assess your ability to classify cognitive objectives. For each of the following cognitive objectives, identify by the appropriate letter the highest level of operation involved: K = knowledge, C = comprehension, AP = application, AN = analysis, S = synthesis, and E = evaluation. Check your answers, and then discuss the results with your peers. Your understanding of the concept involved is more important than whether your score is 100 percent.

_____ 1. Given a poem, the student will recognize the style as being that of Shelley.

_____ 2. Given a list, the student will recognize the misspelled words.

_____ 3. After reading detailed instructions, the student will participate and make a hand puppet.

_____ 4. The student will create a verse using a four-line stanza.

_____ 5. The student will explain his/her critical appraisal of an essay on civil rights.

_____ 6. The student will correctly identify by name the colors shown.

_____ 7. The student will be able to interpret faulty logic in campaign advertising.

_____ 8. Given the political and economic facts, the student will identify a reasonable hypothesis concerning the causes of the riots in Los Angeles.

_____ 9. The student will devise a method to prove that a ray bisects an angle.

_____ 10. Given a list of five solids, five liquids, and five gases, the student will describe the physical and chemical properties of each.

Answer Key

5. E	10. K
4. S	9. S
3. AP	8. AN
2. K	7. E
1. C	6. K

Affective Domain Hierarchy

Krathwohl, Bloom, and Masia developed a useful taxonomy of the affective domain.[3] The following are their major levels (or categories), from least internalized to most internalized:

1. *Receiving.* Being aware of the affective stimulus and beginning to have favorable feelings toward it.
2. *Responding.* Taking an interest in the stimulus and viewing it favorably.
3. *Valuing.* Showing a tentative belief in the value of the affective stimulus and becoming committed to it.
4. *Organizing.* Placing values into a system of dominant and supporting values.
5. *Internalizing.* Demonstrating consistent beliefs and behavior that have become a way of life.

Although there is considerable overlap from one level to another, the hierarchy does give a basis by which to judge the quality of objectives and the nature of learning within the affective domain.

Receiving.   At this level, which is the least internalized, the student exhibits a willingness to give attention to particular phenomena or stimuli, and the teacher is able to arouse, sustain, and direct that attention. Action verbs appropriate for this level include *ask, choose, describe, differentiate, distinguish, hold, identify, locate, name, point to, recall, reply, select,* and *use.*

These are examples of objectives at this level:

• The student will recall the directions for enrichment activities.
• The student will describe the ideas of others.
• The student will identify examples of sensitivity shown to others related to their concerns.

Responding.   At this level, students respond to the stimulus they have received. They may do so because of some external pressure, because they find the stimulus interesting, or because responding gives them satisfaction. Action verbs appropriate for this category include *answer, applaud, approve, assist, command, comply, discuss, greet, help, label, perform, play, practice, present, read, recite, report, select, spend* (leisure time in), *tell,* and *write.*

These are examples of objectives at this level:

• The student will read for enrichment.
• The student will discuss what others have said.
• The student will willingly cooperate with others during group activities.

Valuing.   Objectives at the valuing level deal with a student's beliefs, attitudes, and appreciations. The simplest objectives concern the acceptance of beliefs and values; the higher ones involve learning to prefer certain values and finally becoming committed to them. Action verbs appropriate for this level include *argue, assist, complete, describe, differentiate, explain, follow, form, initiate, invite, join, justify, propose, protest, read, report, select, share, study, support,* and *work.*

These are examples of objectives at this level:

- The student will protest against racial discrimination.
- The student will support actions against gender discrimination.
- The student will argue for or against abortion rights.

Organizing.   The fourth level within the affective domain concerns the building of a personal value system. Here, the student is conceptualizing and arranging values into a system that recognizes their relative importance. Action verbs appropriate for this level include *adhere, alter, arrange, balance, combine, compare, defend, define, discuss, explain, form, generalize, identify, integrate, modify, order, organize, prepare, relate,* and *synthesize.*
    These are examples of objectives at this level:

- The student will form judgments concerning proper behavior in the classroom, school, and community.
- The student will adhere to a personal work ethnic.
- The student will defend the important values of his or her culture.

Internalizing.   At this level, the last and highest within the affective domain, the student's behaviors are consistent with his or her beliefs. Action verbs appropriate for this level include *act, complete, display, influence, listen, modify, perform, practice, propose, qualify, question, revise, serve, solve,* and *verify.*
    These are examples of objectives at this level:

- The student will behave according to a well-defined and ethnical code of behavior.
- The student will display accurate verbal communication.
- The student will practice independently and diligently.

Psychomotor Domain Hierarchy

Whereas classification within the cognitive and affective domains is generally agreed upon, there is less agreement on classification within the psychomotor domain. Originally, the goal for this domain was simply to develop and categorize proficiency in skills, particularly those dealing with gross and fine muscle control. The classification of the domain presented here, however, follows this lead but also includes at its highest level the most creative and inventive behaviors, thus coordinating skills and knowledge from all three domains. Consequently, the objectives are in a hierarchy, developed by Harrow, ranging from simple gross locomotor control to the most creative and complex, requiring originality and fine locomotor control.[4] The following are the major levels of the psychomotor domain:

1. *moving*
2. *manipulating*
3. *communicating*
4. *creating*

Moving.   This involves gross motor coordination. Action verbs appropriate for this level include *adjust, carry, clean, locate, obtain,* and *walk.*

These are examples of objectives at this level:

- The student will jump a rope ten times without missing.
- The student will correctly grasp the driving golf club.
- The student will correctly grasp and carry the microscope to the desk.

Manipulating.   This level involves fine motor coordination. Action verbs appropriate for this level include *assemble, build, calibrate, connect, focus, perform*, and *thread*.
   These are examples of objectives at this level:

- The student will build and fly a kite.
- The student will perform the C scale on the clarinet.
- The student will focus the microscope correctly.

Communicating.   This level involves the communication of ideas and feelings. Action verbs appropriate for this level include *analyze, describe, draw, explain*, and *write*.
   These are examples of objectives at this level:

- The student will demonstrate active listening skills.
- The student will describe his or her feelings about the use of animals for medical research.
- The student will accurately draw what he or she observes on a slide through the microscope.

Creating.   This level, the highest of this and all domains, involves the student's coordination of thinking, learning, and behaving in all three domains. Action verbs appropriate for this level include *create, design*, and *invent*.
   These are examples of objectives at this level:

- The student will write (create) a musical composition.
- The student will choreograph (design) a dance pattern.
- From discarded materials, the student will create an environment for an imaginary animal that he or she has invented.

Using the Taxonomies

Theoretically, the taxonomies are constructed so that students achieve each lower level before moving to the next higher level. But because categories overlap, this theory does not always hold in practice. The taxonomies are important in that they emphasize the various levels to which instruction must aspire. For learning to be worthwhile, you must formulate and teach to objectives from the higher levels of the taxonomies as well as from the lower levels. Student thinking and behaving must be moved from the lowest to the highest levels of operation.

   In using the taxonomies, remember that the point is to formulate the best objectives for the job to be done. The taxonomies provide the mechanism for ensuring that you do not spend a disproportionate amount of time on relatively trivial learning. Writing objectives is essential to the preparation of items that will be useful in the assessment of student learning. As you've surely heard before, the most efficient and effective teaching occurs when you clearly communicate your behavioral expectations to students and then teach toward and assess against those expectations. Your instruction, however, must not be limited to that which can be predicted and expressed in behavioral terms.

C.   Refining Written Objectives

Working Independently

The next step in the process of planning an ITU is for you to polish your written objectives. You even may have to completely rewrite some. To help you critically examine your objectives, gather examples of goals and objectives from various lesson plans and other documents, and then compare the examples to what you have written. Notice that this will also help you refine the ITU that you have planned.

As an overview and *raison d'être* for the unit, you might also write educational goals—especially the ones related to pertinent school, district, and state documents—in order to identify what the unit is about and what the students are to learn related to the documents. An overview of the unit can also be included to indicate what you *hope* the students will learn. If desired by your school, write these goals in behavioral terms and be specific. Write about what understandings the students will develop, what skills will be fostered, and what attitudes and appreciations will be addressed during the unit.

Working with Team Members

During a common planning time, each team member should give every other team member a copy of goals and objectives written independently. Then each member can refine the ITU from that member's point of view as he or she reads and reviews the objectives and goals of the other team members. This process should help the team avoid any confusion in the students' minds when the unit is presented. And it should also help eliminate any overlap that the team considers unnecessary.

D.   Developing Learning Activities

Activities constitute the heart of any unit, including an ITU. An effective teacher develops a pre-ITU activity, initiation activities, ongoing activities, and a culminating activity.

Pre-ITU Activity

A pre-ITU activity is often used to introduce the students to points of view from different disciplines for the first time. Such an introduction does not have to be deadly dull. For example, the teacher and the students might begin a particular study by reading books related to an underlying guiding question (idea/topic/theme), a process that perhaps lasts two days. Then the students might review the ITU's plan, individually reserving "ownership" of some inquiries. Over the next few days, the teacher and the students might approach the unit from the point of view of a particular discipline—perhaps moving on to a different discipline every few days or so.

Suppose the perspective of an archeologist is needed for an ITU. The teacher first introduces questions an archeologist would ask and discuss, and then demonstrates how an archeologist would organize and share information about the topic. To help students understand an archeologist's perspective, the teacher briefly and succinctly introduces knowledge and skills unique to that discipline. For instance, a teacher might do this by using excerpts from the book *You Can Be a Woman Egyptologist* by Betsy M. Bryan and Judith L. Cohen (Cascade Press, 1993, grades 4–6). In this work, an Egyptologist explains how she became interested in the profession, what work she does, and what discoveries she has made. This book is suitable to be read aloud.

Suppose the perspective of a paleontologist is needed for an ITU. The teacher might consider using excerpts from the novel *My Daniel* by Pam Conrad (New York: Harper & Row, 1989, grades 7–8). In this story, eighty-year-old Julia Creath Summerwaite takes her grandchildren to New York's Museum of Natural History to see the dinosaur exhibit. She also tells them about her brother, Daniel, his passion for fossils, and how he engaged in fierce competition with other paleontologists for treasures in Nebraska.

On subsequent days, the teacher can encourage students to see things from the vantage point of various other disciplines—economics, anthropology, history, and so on. Through this process, the teacher gets the students involved in thinking about what can be explored and what inquiries can be made from the perspective of different disciplines. And once the students are introduced to some of the knowledge and skills of different disciplines, they can use what they have learned as they make their own inquiries through an ITU.

One effective way to introduce students to the perspective of a discipline is to encourage them to assume the role of a professional in that discipline as they examine

An ITU can be initiated any number of ways, though the approach taken should be one that will engage the students' interest in the topic. Here, students observe the preparation of a potato for a simulated hydroponics activity.

Anthropology

Taking the role of an anthropologist. The students can ask, "How will our experience(s) in our own culture help us understand the way other people live?" When the students take this role, they show that they are committed to direct observation as the primary way to gather data. They focus on a relationship between people's behaviors and their beliefs. While taking the anthropologist's role, students see each culture as *one* variety of human behavior among the many possibilities and can inquire, "What direct observations can we make to see a relationship about people's behavior and their beliefs?"

Economics

Taking the role of an economist. The students can ask, "What work in the economy is done by people to develop and bring information to us?" The students show that they are interested in the resolution of problems, such as unemployment, that exist in our society. In this role, they also inquire, "What economic problem(s) can be identified?" and "What resolutions of the problem(s) can be suggested?"

Expressive Arts

Taking the role of an artist. The students can ask, "How can we show what we know about the subject through the visual and performing arts, such as art, music, dance, and sculpture?"

Geography

Taking the role of a geographer. The students can ask, "How has geography influenced the topic and what we know about the topic?"

History

Taking the role of an historian. The students can ask, "How has this topic changed over time?" and "How have ways we receive information about the topic changed over time?"

Mathematics

Taking the role of a mathematician. The students can ask, "How can we express what we know about the topic through mathematics?" and "How can mathematics help us learn more about this topic?"

Science

Taking the role of a scientist. The students can ask, "What scientists operate to bring us information about the topic?" and "How can science help us learn more about this?"

Political Science

Taking the role of a political scientist. The students can ask, "How have people organized themselves to provide information about the topic?" In this role, they expand their knowledge about government and politics.

Sociology

Taking the role of a sociologist. The students can ask, "What groups in society operate to bring us information about the topic?" and "In what ways in the community can we participate to resolve a real problem related to the topic?" In this role, they show ways they are committed to understanding aspects of sociology that can give a sense of the relationship between humans and society and a sense of how the world is or is not predictable.

Other Disciplines

Disciplines selected by the students and the teacher.

Figure 3.2 Assuming Roles as a Way to Introduce Students to Various Disciplines

some topic or content. Figure 3.2 might give you some ideas about how to help students take such roles (see also Planning Master 5).

Initiation Activities

An ITU can be initiated by a great variety of activities, ranging from a science learning center to social actions in the community. Patricia Roberts[5] has pointed out that the teacher should decide which of the many beginnings is most appropriate for the students, considering their interests, abilities, and skills. For example, the teacher might start an introduction to a unit's content with an artifact, a book, a computer simulation, or an educational film. Consider some of these approaches to initiate a unit:

displays	learning centers
newspaper articles	paintings
problems	questions
replicas	resource people from the community
role playing	social actions related to the area

A Question Map as a Way to Begin.   To initiate student interest in an ITU, the teacher will want to select an interesting way to launch the unit, one that will arouse the curiosity of the students in the topic. For example, a teacher might fill the classroom environment with materials that will stimulate the students to want to know more about the topic. The teacher could have books related to the topic on display throughout the room to catch students' attention as they come to class. After allowing time to let students browse, the teacher can read aloud a few pages from one or two books and then invite students to ask questions. From those questions, the teacher constructs a web for the unit on the board. The teacher can group the questions in categories and then elicit headings for the groups from the students:

Heading for Questions	**Heading for Questions**	**Heading for Questions**
1. question	1.	1.

Theme: _____

Heading for Questions	**Heading for Questions**	**Heading for Questions**
1.	1.	1.

As a student asks a question or makes a suggestion, the teacher allows the student to reserve that area for his or her own special inquiry. The teacher might also reserve a special topic for inquiry, too. Both teacher and students then begin the unit with some research on some of the most prominent aspects of the topic, using the books the teacher has made available throughout the room.

Ongoing Activities

Once the ITU has been initiated, the students become occupied with a variety of ongoing activities. In doing these activities, the students integrate reading, writing, and art activities. The teacher might engage the students in building models of objects related to the ITU theme, using selected materials. Further, the teacher might also assign a homework project related to the unit that requires the students to research the history of something.

The teacher should refer to the learning experiences ladder in planning ongoing activities for an ITU. As the unit progresses, the teacher can observe which subject areas are addressed through each activity.

If there are specific curriculum requirements from the state, district, or school that must be addressed in the ITU, the teacher can reference the requirements by activity in the scope-and-sequence plan. If desired, the teacher may also reference which sections of the state framework, district curriculum document(s), and local school documents are being addressed through each activity. A teacher's notes may look like this:

Activities in Scope-and-Sequence Plan	*State, District, and School Documents as References*
1. activity A	1. reference(s) for A

Third-Grade Examples of Ongoing Activities.   Recently, a third-grade teacher was in a transitional mode in the classroom, gradually changing from a traditional approach of instruction to an integrated one (Traiger, 1993). This teacher introduced a science learning center as a beginning for an ITU about chromatography (the separation of mixtures, often into various colored layers).[6] The unit integrated a number of disciplines, including history, social science, fine art, literature, and mathematics. At the center, the students tested the colors of water-soluble ink markers, making predictions about what colors the ink might separate into. For example, they tested the ink of a green marker (blue and yellow), the ink of an orange marker (red and yellow), the ink of a purple marker (red and blue), and the ink of other markers selected by the students. They recorded their predictions on individual duplicated sheets with headings similar to the following:

Ink I Used	*What I Predicted*	*What I Observed*
1. green		
2. orange		
3. purple		
4. other		

With strips of paper towels, the students folded each strip so that it hung from the rim of a glass, just touching the inside bottom. Once the strips were folded to the correct length, the students marked a band of color about two inches up from the bottom of each strip. After placing a marked strip in the glass, students would add about 1 inch of water. They then observed what happened as the water moved up the strip and into the colored band, recording the results in their science journals. Here are some examples of how this activity was related to various disciplines:

- *Art.* The students put colors on coffee filters and redid their color experiment. They then cut different shapes from the filters to mount on a class mural in order to demonstrate what colors the different inks separated into during their experiments. Insect and other animal shapes were cut from the filters, and the teacher suggested that the students glue those shapes to paper. Drawings were added that camouflaged the creatures, showing the effectiveness or lack of effectiveness some of the colors might have in protecting living things from danger.
- *Ecology.* The camouflage activity was used to initiate further study about rain forest habitats and the camouflage used by living creatures there.

- *History*. The students were asked to research individuals in history who had been protected by camouflage.
- *Language arts*. The students were asked to consider a situation in which a series of ink spots was found on a piece of clothing and then create a mystery/detective story about what happened and who did it.

The teacher introduced books related to the ITU. *Hide and Snake* by Keith Baker (New York: Harcourt, 1991) was introduced so the students could see how a snake hid near familiar objects in a game of hide and seek. A nature hunt was reviewed using *How to Hide a Butterfly and Other Insects* by Ruth Heller (New York: Grossett & Dunlap, 1985). The teacher also showed illustrations on an opaque projector and asked students to locate camouflaged bees, butterflies, inchworms, and other hidden creatures.

At various intervals, different color experiments and activities were introduced to the science center, such as placing celery in food dye to observe the movement of molecules caused by capillary actions, learning the technique of marbleizing paper, and using litmus paper to determine if a substance is acidic or basic. As a related activity, the students were asked to construct three pairs of eyeglasses with ear frames, using heavy art paper. The lenses (color filters) were made from red, yellow, and blue cellophane. They were asked to observe items through the different color filters and predict what would happen to the color of the items when viewed through the different filters. They recorded their predictions on a journal page with these headings:

Colored Item I Selected   *What I Predicted*   *What I Observed*

1.

A table display of books related to color included *Color Dance* by Ann Jonas (Greenwillow, 1989), in which dancers demonstrate what happens when red and yellow (and other colors) are mixed. Arnold Lobel's *The Great Blueness and Other Predicaments* (New York: Harper & Row, 1968) described a colorful world about a wizard and his paint pots and explored why the red mice that once lived with blue trees, yellow ice, and black cheese disappeared. *Mouse Paint* by Ellen Stoll (New York: Harcourt, Brace, Jovanovich, 1989) introduced color concepts through the actions of three mice. The mice cavort in and out of red, yellow, and blue paint, making paint puddles; in doing so, they discover the colors green, orange, and purple.

At the beginning of the chromatography unit, the teacher captured students' attention with the development of a question map, a useful way to initiate an ITU. Now turn your attention to Exercise 3.2, Initiating an ITU with a Question Map. You will have the experience of recording questions on a question map, just as you would do in your own classroom. Then do Exercise 3.3, Developing Generalizations, in which you will be asked to write generalizations related to a theme.

Then turn your attention to Exercise 3.4, Connecting Questions and Activities for an ITU, to identify investigations that could prove useful in inquiring about the questions. To assist you in clarifying your own concept of inquiry, make a search for resources (related to the questions developed earlier) by completing Exercise 3.5, Personal Inquiry: Using Questions and Resources and Recording Data. Then move on to Exercise 3.6, Reviewing Your Personal Inquiry. This exercise allows you to reflect upon what you did in the previous exercises. In Exercise 3.7, Putting Objectives, Resources, and Learning Activities Together for a Teaching Plan, you are asked to write a specific teaching plan.

EXERCISE 3.2

Initiating an ITU with a Question Map

• • • • • •

Instructions.   The purpose of this exercise is to work with a partner or partners to write questions related to a theme you identified in Chapter 2.

   With your partners taking the role of students, have your partners participate in a discussion about "what we want to know" about the theme. Write their questions on a question map on the writing board. Show the partners how you can group their related questions (main questions and subquestions) together. Ask them to think of headings for the different categories of related questions. Use the following format for recording the input:

1. Theme:

2. Main question:

3. Related subquestions:

   a.

   b.

   c.

Copy the question map from the board to this page so you can use it as a reference.

EXERCISE 3.3
Developing Generalizations

• • • • • •

Instructions.   The purpose of this exercise is to work with a partner or partners to identify concepts and write generalizations from the questions and subquestions generated in Exercise 3.1.

1. Ask your partners to take the role of students. Read each of their questions again, underlining the words in each that identify a concept that will need to be reinforced in your teaching. Have your partners participate in a discussion about any generalizations they can determine from the main concept words. Write the generalizations below:

2. With your partners, read each generalization again, underlining words in each that identify a concept that will need to be reinforced in your teaching. Select one or more of the concepts and discuss ways you can reinforce the concept in your teaching.

EXERCISE 3.4

Connecting Questions and Activities for an ITU

• • • • • •

Instructions.   The purpose of this exercise is to work to connect the questions related to your theme and to learning activities in specific detail. Learning activities should be planned around some central questions (and subquestions) about the theme. The investigative activities that are needed to inquire about the questions can provide various opportunities for you to respond to the learning styles and needs of your students.

With your partners, return to the "what we want to know" question map you completed in Exercise 3.2. Use the information to design some learning activities for the unit. (Figure 1.4 in Chapter 1 shows examples of questions and related activities.)

List of Learning Activities Related to the Questions and Subquestions:

1.

2.

3.

4.

5.

6.

EXERCISE 3.5

Personal Inquiry—Using Questions and Resources and Recording Data

• • • • • •

Instructions.   The purpose of this exercise is to help you clarify your own concept of inquiry. In this exercise, you will locate resources related to the main question and subquestions you developed in Exercise 3.2 and then record relevant data in those resources.

1. Take the role of a student in your classroom engaged in independent inquiry. Reread your question and subquestions, and then list any resources that you think will help you answer those questions.

Resources:

2. Select one (or more) of the questions and collect information from the resources you listed to help you answer the question(s) you wrote related to your thematic study. Begin your search by consulting the sources you listed. Then consult other sources you find in the process.

Date   *Sources Consulted*

3. Keep a record of your personal inquiry (as you might ask students in your class to do) by recording the information you find, your interpretations of the information, and the sources that verify your information.

Question 1:   *Theme Study*

   Information Found

   Interpretation

   Source Used

                                    Question 2:

   Information Found

   Interpretation

   Source Used

                                    Question 3:

   Information Found

   Interpretation

   Source Used

Question 4:

Information Found

Interpretation

Source Used

4. What new questions came to mind as you collected information from the resources? Record any new questions, as well as any hunches, guesses, or predictions you have about the question(s) and the theme of the study.

New Questions:

Hunches, Guesses, Predictions:

With your partner(s), discuss your new questions and your hunches, guesses, and predictions.

EXERCISE 3.6
Reviewing Your Personal Inquiry

• • • • • •

Instructions.   The purpose of this exercise is to take the time to reflect upon the experience you had during your personal inquiry. This effort may help you understand more clearly what goes on during a student's individual inquiry in your classroom.

1. With your partner(s), review the thinking activities you used in your inquiry—what you thought about, what you did, and so on. Discuss what was rewarding and pleasurable about following your interest and what was not. Discuss what you gained from this exercise that helped you understand the idea of individual inquiry related to a theme. Take notes on the discussion in the following section.

2. What ideas do you have for maintaining student interest in your classroom when they are doing independent inquiry?

3. What helped you gain insight into such individual inquiry?

EXERCISE 3.7

Putting Objectives, Resources, and Learning Activities Together for a Teaching Plan

• • • • • •

Instructions.   The purpose of this exercise is to write a specific teaching plan for a minimum of one day that incorporates what you have done so far—writing objectives, selecting resources, and planning learning activities. You may want to reference the learning activities to state frameworks, district documents, and local school curriculum. Ask a peer to read and react to your teaching plan. Does your plan convey what you intended to say? What new questions came to mind as you wrote the plan?

Sample Teaching Plan
Interdisciplinary Unit Theme:

Main Question:

Related subquestions:

Objectives
(What will the students learn?)

(What thinking skills such as observing, communicating, comparing, categorizing, inferring, applying, will the students develop?)

(What affective attitudes will be fostered?)

Resources
(Audiovisuals, artifacts, computer software)

Specifics of Learning Activities

Evaluation

Check √ Discipline Areas Drawn Upon:

____   1. Sciences

____   2. Social Sciences

____   3. Mathematics

____   4. Reading and Language

____   5. Poetry and Prose

____   6. Music and Dance

____   7. Painting and Sculpture

____   8. Health and Physical Education

Other:

Feedback:

1. What was the reaction of your peer to your teaching plan?

2. In your opinion, did your plan convey what you originally envisioned?

3. What new questions came to mind as you wrote the plan?

ITU Culminating Activity

An effective ITU comes to some kind of closure with a culminating activity. Such an activity might involve discussing, evaluating, experimenting, observing, organizing, traveling on field trips, reporting, or developing a product. The teacher could accept the students' suggestions for a culminating activity if it engages them in summarizing what they have learned with others. A culminating activity that brings closure to a unit can give the students an opportunity for synthesis (by assembling, constructing, creating, inventing, producing, or incorporating something) and even an opportunity to present that synthesis to an audience. We mention closure here because of the reality of the academic day and year—the teacher needs to consider the school calendar, the report card periods, and the interests of the students, as well as resources that are available and their effects on the students' inquiry and instruction.

With a culminating activity, the teacher can provide an opportunity for the students to move from recording information to reporting on their learning. For example, one activity might be for students to take field trips to study something related to the theme and then synthesize their learning after the trip in a way that culminates the study. On field trips, students should be given notepads similar to the ones reporters use and asked to take notes and make sketches of what they learn. They can discuss what questions they have on the ride to the site. They can discuss what they liked and did not like on the ride back to school. After the trip, each student can choose something he or she saw and then build it to scale, so the students can have a scale model of something they saw on the trip that caught their interest. Teacher and students might devote one full afternoon, or more, to working with rulers, yardsticks, cardboard, clay, and other materials. The students could then invite other classes in to examine the scale models and listen to student reports about why an object caught their interest. Students might also present an art show of drawings about the unit's theme, with a narration that informs others about their study. The teacher might also schedule a culminating activity that asks students to report on individual projects—the aspect each student formerly reserved for individual study.

Olé! This culminating activity provides students with a fun and interesting way to end a unit on Mexico.

advertisements	fables and myths	poetry
art works	fairy tales and folk tales	posters
albums and books	family trees	puppets
book jackets	filmstrips and slides	puppet shows
bulletin boards	graphs and charts	rubbings
card and board games	greeting cards	scrapbooks, sketches
collages	illustrations for stories	sculptures
comic strips	labeled diagrams	scripts for skits
costumes	letters, diaries, journals	songs and instruments
correspondence to newspapers	maps and murals	stencils
dances	mobiles, models, musical items	stitchery
dioramas	new math problems	tape recordings
displays	pamphlets and flyers	time lines
dramas	pantomimes	transparencies
essays	pop-up books	video recording

Figure 3.3   Means for Culminating Activities

Examples of actual culminating activies are endless. At the end of an interdisciplinary thematic unit taught by a team of teachers (mathematics, science, social studies, and reading), seventh graders developed an Earthquake Safety Guide.[7] At North Middle School, O'Fallon, Missouri, an interdisciplinary thematic study about immigrants, called All Americans, involved four teachers (mathematics, history, science, and English). The immigrant experience came alive for students as they assumed an identity and received an official document containing visas for the unit. During the unit students went through processing and naturalization as an "immigrant," encountering the problems and prejudices faced daily by many immigrants. In the culminating activity for this unit, the "immigrants" became naturalized citizens by completing a required assignment, including a group presentation, a spreadsheet and graph, a fairy tale, and a natural resources map.[8]

Culminating activities are opportunities for the students to contribute what they have learned in different and individual ways. The teacher should encourage the students to use a variety of means for presenting what was learned—perhaps a tour of a community resource, a simulated museum exhibit, a learning "fair," or a multimedia presentation that includes the use of the computer, films, videos, and audio tapes. We suggest several means in Figure 3.3.

Now gain insight into how to bring an ITU to closure by doing Exercise 3.8, Planning Culminating Activities.

EXERCISE 3.8
Planning Culminating Activities

• • • • • •

Instructions.   The purpose of this exercise is to plan a closure for the unit (even though you realize that inquiry can be life long and has no official closure). In this exercise, you must determine what will affect the length of your unit—the interest of your students in the topic, the resources that are available or unavailable, the school holidays, the academic calendar for your school year, and any competing events, such as picture day, assemblies and athletic events, and field trips.

1. What activity/activities could you plan that would permit your students to synthesize what they have learned in the unit and then report the synthesis to a selected audience?

2. Which of the following would you incorporate into the culmination of a unit? Explain why.

   Creating new problems related to the topic and demonstrating a way to resolve them.

   Demonstrating computer software related to the topic.

   Designing a chart, map, time line, classroom museum of exhibits, an interdisciplinary thematic fair, or a classroom "main street" with booths (learning centers), and reporting on the data the design represents.

Making an oral presentation on an aspect of the topic; using such creative ways to present data as sketches, sculpture works, cartoons, popular songs, a comic strip format, costume props, a story board, puppets, flannel board figures, rhymes, limericks, and other forms of poetry.

Producing an act in a play, a musical composition, or new lyrics for a familiar tune.

Reporting on interviews with other people.

Writing a letter or entries in a learning log or educational diary.

Writing a report related to the topic.

Writing and publishing a newsletter or brochure on the topic.

Writing and publishing an individual book.

Writing and publishing a cooperative-group book.

Writing and publishing a whole-group book.

Writing and publishing a scientific article.

E.   Meeting the Needs and Abilities of a Diversity of Students

The researchers Cohen, de Avila, and Intili (1981) have pointed out that an important aspect of instruction is to foster equal status among students in the classroom—that is, to raise the classroom social status of lower achievers. Their studies, based on what the researchers call *expectation states theory*, indicate that to accomplish their goal learning in the classroom is best presented across a broad front—through a wide variety of activities. The theory provides a foundation for teaching techniques and classroom organizational plans that relate to the students working independently, teaming collaboratively with others, and cooperating in small learning groups. For example, one fourteen-week study daily exposed students in nine classes (grades 2, 3, and 4) to a wide range of activities in addition to the students' basic course of study. The activities, presented daily in half-hour and hour segments as special instruction, were designed to improve the students' academic, cognitive, and linguistic skills. The results of this study are discussed in the sections that follow.

Students Working Independently

To raise the classroom social status of lower achievers, the teachers in the study gave special instruction to such students prior to their participation in cooperative learning groups. This instruction included a brief discussion about the various and unique abilities that would be required for the tasks in group work. The teachers tried to instill the idea that each student has different skills and abilities needed during the group work. They emphasized that all skills and abilities would be needed and therefore each student would be "good" on at least one of the group tasks. The teachers then talked with these students about differences in working with others and working alone.

Students Teamed with Others

During that discussion, students came to understand that each student could ask anyone in his or her group for help and that every student would help anyone who asked for help. The teachers let the students know that after they finished their task(s) in their small groups or at a learning center, they could choose a new group or center in which to work. Students then practiced asking questions of one another, role-playing ways of giving assistance when asked. They practiced ways to explain things to others and ways of showing someone how something works. They acted out or discussed some of the responsibilities related to the role of the group members assigned by the teacher. Figure 3.4 shows some common roles used in group learning.

Cooperating in Learning Groups

In the small groups, verbal interaction—student talking—was emphasized. In fact, the focus on verbal interaction was a critical element in the group work. Several pertinent features were noted by the teachers, including talking about the group's tasks, asking for assistance, and offering assistance to others. Verbal interaction also included talking to the teacher or a classroom aide, as well as non-task-related conversation. There seemed to be a substantial relationship between the percentage of time that the students were observed talking and their educational gains (de Avila, Cohen, & Intili, 1981).

In addition to the verbal interactions, other social actions were observed, such as wandering around (usually at transition time), working alone, observing others, and

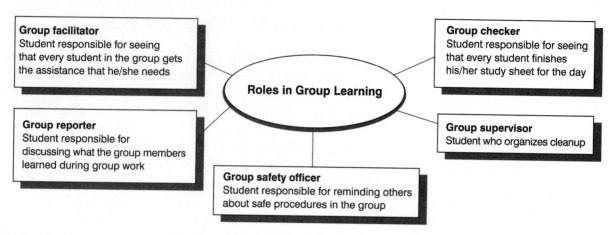

Figure 3.4.   Sample Roles in Group Learning

time spent waiting for directions. Some teachers find that allowing the students in small groups to make decisions about the task procedures gives them a sense of empowerment and self-control and provides opportunities to develop active citizenship skills—a major goal for a democratic society (Cohen, 1986). Furthermore, Donald Graves has pointed out (in Hoskisson & Thompkins, 1987) that cooperating in small groups helps the students become more independent as learners (in contrast to students who depend mainly on the teacher as a source of knowledge).

During this group work, it appeared that a daily study-sheet activity significantly contributed to the gains of the students. There seemed to be a strong relationship between the amount of time the student spent with the study sheets and improvement in reading and math—the academic focus of the study. These gains were later seen on the scores of the students on the California Test of Basic Skills (CTBS). Thus, the study sheets seemed to be powerful reinforcers of the instruction of basic skills.

These study sheets were designed so that the information required from the students could be given without any written language (drawings were used), and thus this activity did not penalize a student who lacked the appropriate oral or written language proficiencies. The study sheets, to be filled out in English, Spanish, or another target language, included procedures that were drawn, and the responses from the students could also be drawn. Further, it seemed that in order for new material to be usefully absorbed into the students' memories, the material had to be discussed and talked about with other students. Overall, the proficient bilingual students were the ones who showed the most consistent improvements.

Through instruction in an interdisciplinary thematic unit, the students can be organized in a broad range of teaching and learning arrangements, including independent work, teaming with others, and cooperating in small learning groups. Additional arrangements include learning centers and teaching mini-lessons to one or more students, student partners, various small groups, and the whole group.

Now that you have considered the value of a variety of learning activities, turn your attention again to the learning activities you want to include in an ITU. In Exercise 3.4 you were asked to plan your learning activities around some central questions (and subquestions) about a theme. Now do Exercise 3.9, Identifying Intellectual Processes, Disciplines, and Learning Styles of Students in the Learning Activities. This exercise will give you an opportunity to see how professionally attuned you have become to these facets of learning activities.

EXERCISE 3.9

Identifying Intellectual Processes, Disciplines, and Learning Styles of Students in the Learning Activities

• • • • • •

Instructions.   The purpose of this exercise is to review your learning activities in more specific detail. In Exercise 3.4, you were asked to plan your learning activities around some central questions (and subquestions) about the theme. The activities that were needed to inquire about the questions can provide various opportunities for you to identify the related intellectual processes, discipline and subject areas, and the learning styles and needs of your students.

1. Return to the learning activities you wrote in Exercise 3.4 and identify the intellectual processes in the cognitive domain—knowledge, comprehension, application, analysis, synthesis, and evaluation—that are mainly emphasized in each activity. Identify these critical-thinking processes by abbreviations used in Exercise 3.1.

2. Review the learning activities again and identify the disciplines emphasized in each activity.

3. Return to your learning activities again and identify the learning styles of students emphasized in each activity. Identify these by the abbreviations of these learning styles:

   symbolic emphasis (*sy*), which indicates the activities asking students to think with symbol systems such as words and numerals.

   imaging (*im*), which indicates the activities asking students to learn through visual or kinesthetic approaches.

   affect (*af*), which indicates the activities incorporating feelings and emotions that could motivate students' inquiries.

4. Give your list of learning activities to another member in your class and ask him or her to review the identifications you made for each activity to see if you have addressed a variety of intellectual processes, disciplines, and learning styles to meet the needs of your students.

Summary

In this chapter, you were asked to use your skills further and write objectives, select resources, and plan learning activities for a minimum period of time. Through a review of the learning activities, you were engaged in identifying intellectual processes, disciplines, subject areas and learning styles and needs of the students. It was suggested that the ITU close with a final activity that allows the students to share what they have learned and display what their skills have produced during the unit. We pointed out that a teacher can choose from a variety of beginnings and activities for a unit and choose specific areas of the curriculum to include in the study. Additionally, we reviewed expectation states theory (Cohen, 1978, 1979), a theory that can provide a foundation underpinning for teaching techniques and classroom organizational plans that relate to the students working independently, teaming with others, and cooperating in small learning groups. Chapter 3 also suggested that you engage in a simulation with others in the activity of developing a question map to initiate a unit, that you use the questions to identify concept words and write generalizations related to the unit, and that you link the questions to appropriate learning activities. On a personal note, you were asked to participate in a personal inquiry and reflect about the experience.

Chapter Notes

1. This description was contributed by Kristie Darras, a second-grade teacher in the Elk Grove Unified School District, Elk Grove, California.
2. Rather than an orderly progression from simple to complex mental operations as illustrated by Bloom's taxonomy, other researchers prefer an organization of cognitive abilities that ranges from simple information storage and retrieval through a higher level of discrimination and concept attainment, to the highest cognitive ability to recognize and solve problems; see Robert M. Gagne, Leslie Briggs, and Walter Wager, *Principles of Instructional Design*, 3rd Ed. (New York: Holt, Rinehart and Winston, 1988).
3. David R. Krathwohl, Benjamin S. Bloom, and Bertram B. Masia, *Taxonomy of Educational Goals: Handbook 2, Affective Domain* (New York: David McKay, 1964).
4. For a deeper discussion of this domain, see A. J. Harrow's *Taxonomy of the Psychomotor Domain* (New York: Longman, 1977).
5. Patricia Roberts, *A Green Dinosaur Day: A Guide for Developing Thematic Units in Literature-Based Instruction, K–6* (New York: Allyn & Bacon, 1993).
6. This unit on color is based on an article in *California Catalyst* (1993) by Karen Traiger, San Jose Unified School District, San Jose, California.
7. See the guide in Richard D. Kellough and Noreen G. Kellough, *Middle School Teaching: Methods and Resources* (Englewood Cliffs, NJ: Merrill/Prentice Hall, 1996).
8. For further information regarding the All Americans unit, contact Nancy Bergfeld, Mike Crain, Dana Humphrey, or Mike Lesch at North Middle School, 210 Virgil, O'Fallon, Missouri 63366 (Phone 314-272-6620, ext. 270).

Questions and Activities for Discussion

1. What suggestions do you have for the use of ITUs with diverse populations, i.e., gifted and talented students, students who are at risk of dropping out of school, stu-

dents who have limited proficiency in English, and students who have special needs? What resources will help you find out more about this? As one sample source, related to working with gifted children, read "The Interdisciplinary Concept Model: Theory and Practice," by H. H. Jacobs and J. H. Borland in *Gifted Child Quarterly*, in which the authors suggest a multi-step approach to thematic study for gifted children. Report your findings to the group.

2. How would you develop objectives for an interdisciplinary lesson for an ITU for a classroom of diverse students? In small groups, review the lesson you planned for a classroom of multicultural students (see "Questions and Activities for Discussion" at the end of Chapter 2). You might begin by brainstorming objectives about aspects of the lesson and then correlate the appropriate objectives to the lesson. Identify the action verbs in the objectives.

3. In small groups, discuss the complex and challenging tasks of collaborative learning, risk-taking, developing hypotheses, and creating visual graphics (such as question maps) as teaching and learning processes that can be a part of an ITU approach. Each member of the group can be responsible for presenting information about one of the tasks. Discuss the uses of each one, and if time allows, any abuses you know about from your experience.

Individual Notes

Chapter

. . . .

4

Assessing and Evaluating

. . . .

Everything should be made as simple as possible, but not simpler.

—*Albert Einstein*

. . . .

INTERDISCIPLINARY THEMATIC UNIT FOR MIDDLE SCHOOL STUDENTS: *AFRICAN AMERICANS—JOURNEY TO FREEDOM*

In the early 1990s, teachers Janet Hickman and Rudine Sims Bishop (1993) addressed multicultural education through an interdisciplinary thematic study of African-American history for middle school students. In the unit they developed, these teachers linked historical issues related to the theme with such disciplines as music, science, and sociology. The use of expressive language and other skills was taught along with the content.

This thematic study approached African-American history through a variety of activities related to several disciplines. Students had a choice to involve themselves in one or more of those activities, including:

- *Music.* Students could sing or listen to spirituals or develop appropriate accompaniment for various spirituals.
- *Science.* Students could use biographies and other reference materials to write nominations for the students' African American Hall of Fame, which would include scientists, inventors, entrepreneurs, and so on. Arguments could be presented for candidates, and the class could vote for a Top 5 or Top 10 and display photocopies of candidates on the bulletin board.

- *Language Arts.* Students could collect the work(s) of an African American illustrator, author, or poet, or they could interview relatives and neighbors to collect stories of holidays and such family traditions as celebrating Kwanzaa.
- *History.* Students could compare one chapter in a book, by Walter Dean Myers such as *Now Is Your Time: The African American Struggle for Freedom* (New York: HarperCollins, 1991), with material about the same time period in a standard history text. In another activity related to history, a student could assume the role of an historical figure presented in relevant material and hold a news conference, with other class members acting as reporters. Students then could compose newspaper articles from their notes.
- *Sociology.* Students could compare stories of African American families (and communities) written recently with similar stories written in the past, noting differences in society and personal attitudes.

In Chapter 3 we pointed out that a teacher can move across the curriculum to provide various opportunities for students to develop their skills. We also reviewed teaching techniques and classroom organizational plans related to students working independently, teaming with others, and cooperating in small groups. We emphasized that the classroom social status of a student affects a student's interaction and that this interaction then affects the amount of learning that occurs during a specific unit.

In the exercises of Chapter 3 you developed a question map that could initiate a unit, used questions to identify concept words and write generalizations related to the unit, and connected the questions to appropriate learning activities. In addition, you carried out a personal inquiry and reflected upon that experience. You also

- wrote objectives, selected resources, and planned learning activities.
- identified intellectual processes, disciplines, and learning styles of the students.
- considered a culminating activity that would allow students to share what they learned and display what they produced during the unit.

In this chapter, we turn our attention to various assessment techniques, so you can discover what your students are learning (assessment) and then compare that with what you want them to be learning as stated in your objectives (evaluation).

A.   Assessment Techniques

By now you probably understand that students' personal inquiries are central to an ITU. And you probably have inferred that much of the assessment of student work must be done through an informal and continuous process. All through the academic day, a teacher will observe students and make judgments about the quality and quantity of their work. For example, a teacher will note which individual students are having what type of problems or which students need what type of assistance to make progress in their learning. As a teacher circulates around the classroom with note cards or a form, he or she can assess the status of individual students and groups, as related to expectation states theory (see Chapter 3). And as a teacher observes the work of the students, he or she can decide what teaching needs to be done through individual instruction, small-group work, or whole-group instruction and respond to what deficiencies are showing up in the students' work.

Some teachers record their notes on small adhesive-backed papers, later affixing those notes in anecdotal notebooks by the appropriate students' names. A teacher's observations and informal methods of assessment are central to the evaluation of learning. Thus, a teacher will want to establish carefully annotated records for each student so the progress of learning is reported accurately. A variety of assessment techniques can be useful in establishing accurate reports, and we discuss a number of them in the following sections.

Portfolios

A portfolio is a collection of a student's writing samples, as well as other evidence of that student's progress in learning.[1] Often, a file folder, three-ring binder, or notebook is used to organize the student's work and to hold the teacher's written observations. In some classrooms, the teacher requires a copy of the goals for the course of study and the objectives for the ITU to be kept in the portfolio. When goals and objectives are included, they are most useful when used as an educational inventory checklist. This means that the documents placed in the portfolio are examples of the students' performance related to the goals and objectives. The inventory checklist might have columns such as these:

Goals and Objectives   *Student Documents Related to Goals/Objectives*
   1.   1.
   2.   2.

The documents called for in the right-hand column would be ones that show the student's acquisition, mastery, and maintenance of skills during the ITU. These could include examples of homework, in-class assignments, individual inquiry, and creative projects.

Some teachers use the portfolio as a "triad" project, with students, parents, and teacher each contributing one-third of the documents to the portfolio. For example, a student would select one-third of the material to be inserted and his or her parents or guardians would select another third from work sent home. The parents or guardians could bring the material to school at a mutually agreed-upon conference time. The teacher selects the remaining one-third. The purpose of a portfolio is to provide a means for continuous assessment. Materials kept in the portfolio show how a student has acquired, improved, or maintained skills through such items as drafts and revisions of reports, letters, memos, brief essays, descriptive paragraphs, artwork, charts, graphs, and word webs.

Filing work in the portfolios benefits both the students and the teacher. For the students, keeping their work in the portfolios involves them in ownership, gives them a sense of accomplishment as they set future goals, and opens the door to their participation in the evaluation process. For the teacher, keeping students' work in portfolios allows the teacher to examine growth and the development of skills over the length of the unit, helps the teacher assess student and curriculum needs, and improves the one-to-one communication between the teacher and the individual student. For both, keeping the work in portfolios helps the teacher and the students work together to set future goals, links the process of learning to various products that are created, and is a basis for cooperative assessment.[2] Now explore your own understanding of portfolios by doing Exercise 4.1, Assessment through the Use of Portfolios.

EXERCISE 4.1

Assessment through the Use of Portfolios

• • • • • •

Instructions.   The purpose of this exercise is to explore one way of assessing your students' learning as they participate in their inquiries through an interdisciplinary thematic unit. Portfolios are quite useful in assessing the students' progress, because the teacher can collect information over the length of the unit. You should encourage the students to use their portfolios as a repository for their work—especially for their best work—and for descriptions or drawings of what they did (how they learned) that will show or describe the processes in which they were engaged.

Now explore your own understanding of portfolios by answering the following questions.

1. What materials do you think should be included in a student's portfolio that will show that the student has gained some relevant information related to the topic?

2. What materials do you think should be included in a student's portfolio that will show that the student has developed and used various thinking processes (observing, classifying, etc.) related to the topic?

3. What materials do you think should be included in a student's portfolio that will show that the student has used a variety of resources in his or her inquiry?

4. Reread what you wrote in earlier exercises about the learning activities that you would want to include in an interdisciplinary thematic unit and determine what materials would be produced from those activities. Which of the materials would you want placed in a portfolio?

Anecdotal Records

An anecdotal record is usually written in a notebook where a teacher keeps a profile of observations of students related to their progress in learning. For example, a teacher who decides to keep a profile on the learning and writing of students may ask that each Friday the students write a brief report about "Something I Learned in the ITU This Week." The teacher can then examine each student's sample to look for any patterns that emerge over time and for what learning experience each student reports.

Audio and Video Recordings

Audio or video recordings can be very helpful for a student to use in the self-assessment of his or her progress in class discussions, reading aloud, creative drama and role play, and other speaking situations and instructional activities. Such self-assessment should be done in a private setting, where a student can listen to or watch a recording of a classroom activity.

Some teachers record each student several times during the unit to have a record of each student's reading progress related to the unit of study. In reviewing the recordings, the teacher can identify which reading strategies the student is or is not using and plan future individual or small-group instruction accordingly.

Audio or video recordings can be useful in other situations, too. Consider some of the following:

Students in a study group audiotape their ideas and then transcribe them for other groups.

Students take dictation from a group's discussion on a tape.

Students act in the role of recorders and listen to or watch a tape of a small-group meeting and then make a hard copy of the important ideas for the whole group.

Checklists

A checklist, developed by the students, the teacher, or both, is a collection of specific points that can provide evidence of either the presence or absence of a particular behavior, trait, ability, or characteristic under consideration. For example, the students might cooperatively develop a checklist of points important for giving oral reports related to an ITU or a checklist of points about the behavior of members in the audience. A teacher might develop a checklist for use in recording his or her observations of the students as they participate in activities during the unit. Examples of how checklists can be incorporated into a variety of activities are discussed in the sections that follow.

Listening to a Story.   One way for a teacher to assess listening skills is to ask a student to retell a story related to the unit topic that has previously been read aloud by the teacher. The teacher listens to the retelling with a checklist in hand that includes entries related to understanding the sense of text, knowing the structure of the story, and recognizing various story elements—setting, beginning events, actions of the main character, reactions, and outcomes. In that way, the teacher can observe the extent to which a student demonstrates how well he or she had listened to the original story.

Listening to an Audio Selection.   A teacher could have students listen to a variety of sources related to the unit topic—live newscasts, talk radio, recorded debates and speeches, segments from television and videos, and so on—and evaluate the central message of each. As a group, the class could first discuss the basic elements of good listening and reporting—who, what, where, when and why. Then, as the students respond to the audio selections, the teacher can observe the extent to which each student has a sense of those basic elements. Using a checklist, the teacher records students' responses to such questions as

- What was the setting?
- What was its importance?
- Who was the speaker and what do you know about the speaker?
- What was the speaker presenting?
- What was the reason the material was presented?
- Who was listening in the audience?
- Did the speaker's words affect you?
- Why or why not?

Participating in Group Work.   A teacher might engage them in group work and then record notes of the students' involvement in their study tasks. A teacher's checklist of notes about student participation could include items related to how well a student

- helps others
- makes decisions
- collects and records information
- discusses the topic
- helps organize material collected by the group
- helps draw conclusions from the information
- prepares materials for presenting the group's findings
- participates in making a presentation about the group's findings to the whole class
- helps make a positive contribution to the purpose of the group.

A teacher can use a checklist to help assess students' participation in group work.

Speaking Out About a Topic.   A teacher could have a small group of students sit in a circle and give opinions about a topic related to an ITU. Another small group encircles the first group and observes the discussion. While the students in the inner circle speak out about a topic, the students in the outer circle assess the discussion with a peer-developed checklist that has been previously approved by the two groups. For example, such a checklist could include such questions as

- Which student seemed interested in the discussion? Most interested?
- What language used by a student affected or impressed you the most?
- Who used the most clever language? The most powerful language?
- From your point of view, which suggestions were good ones? Why?
- Which student seemed to be listening to the words of the others? What did that student do?
- Which student seemed to be best communicating his or her thoughts about the topic? How did the student show this?

In addition to reviewing such peer-assessment checklists, the teacher can also be an active observer, making notes about the way students use oral language, the way the students communicate their thoughts about the topic, and the way different students participate in the discussion.

Reading about a Topic.   A teacher could encourage students to self-select what they want to read on a topic. Once the reading has been done, individual students prepare for a conference with the teacher by writing some answers to a self-evaluation checklist. The checklist, to be discussed in the conference, could include such questions as

- Why did I select this book on the topic?
- What made the reading easy or difficult to understand?
- Was this book a good choice? Why or why not?
- What did I learn from the book?
- What were the important points in the book?

When the students are reading aloud in groups, the teacher could observe the students' participation in the group and note particular reading behaviors. Those reading behaviors could be recorded on a checklist prepared by the teacher. For instance, a teacher will want to know if a student can locate information in the reading text, if a student can make use of information, and if a student can use the context to clarify the meaning of what is being read. A teacher also will want to note which students can analyze words and meanings and which students know the value of using charts, headings, illustrations, captions, and maps as reading aids.

Writing Conventions.   A teacher could use a transparency to show several handwriting examples on an overhead projector. The students could then be asked to assess their own handwriting progress with a checklist, indicating what handwriting goals they plan for themselves in the future. This brief self-assessment might be included in their portfolios. Such a handwriting checklist can include such questions as

- Does the writing stay on the base line?
- Can one letter be recognized from another?

- Are the capital letters even?
- Are the small letters even?
- Does the spacing look even?
- Is the writing slant the same?

Now develop your skill in composing a checklist by doing Exercise 4.2, Developing a Checklist for Assessment.

EXERCISE 4.2
Developing a Checklist for Assessment

• • • • • •

Instructions.   The purpose of this exercise is to develop your skill in composing a checklist that would be useful in recording your notes as you observe students. Consider the arrangement of a general checklist form that follows, and then make your own improvements for a checklist you would use in your classroom.

Student _____ Grade _____

School _____

Teacher _____ Date _____ Period _____

Expected Outcomes (Objectives)   *Students' Behavior*

1.

2.

3.

Teacher's Comments

Diaries

In some classrooms students make entries in diaries each day. At the end of a day, the teacher asks class members to summarize the progress they made in studying the unit that day and record that summary in their diaries in order to keep a continuing account of what is being learned in the unit. For example, students involved in a study of Ancient Greece could record what they learned about that time and place at the end of each day. On subsequent days, students can be invited to refer to their diaries in class and group meetings to check on previous activities, decisions, and plans related to Ancient Greece. The diaries could also be the focus of a culminating activity as students recall details of the work that went on.

During the progress of a unit, students could cooperatively agree upon the focus of the daily entries in their diaries. Students might agree to make entries for what facts were learned, what new approaches were tried, what each student did "best," which students were work partners, and what specific ways the students spent their academic time.

Journals

A journal (sometimes called a learning log) usually takes the form of a spiral notebook that contains a student's writing. In general, journal entries show what is being learned in the ITU. A journal might include personal writing about the student's interests and experiences, in which case it is sometimes called a life-writing journal, or a student's personal reactions to material related to the ITU, in which case it is sometimes called a thinkbook. A journal might also contain entries written by the student every afternoon before leaving school about what was learned that day, in which case it is sometimes called a cooperative teacher-student log.

The teacher can communicate in writing with each student through any of the various types of journals. It is crucial, though, for the teacher to write comments for each student when the approach taken is the cooperative teacher-student log. In this type of log, the student writes about what he or she thinks has been accomplished for the day, what was personally interesting during the day's study, and what he or she wants to read, write, or study next. An effective teacher communicates by reading such logs often and by making meaningful written responses.

If the teacher wants to make the cooperative teacher-student log part of the ITU, the teacher may want to read the logs as part of the overall assessment of the unit and recognize the students for the effort that they put into their journal entries with some type of awards and bonuses. In addition, the students can reread their journals at the end of the ITU, creating an end-of-the-unit review of what they have learned after rereading their entries. The students might number the journal pages, write titles for the different entries on different pages, create a table of contents page, decorate a cover and a title page, develop a glossary or index, and write a self-evaluation as a summary on the last page of the journal to establish a closure for the ITU.

Writing Folders

A writing folder is usually a three-ring binder containing a number of cardboard pockets, labeled to show the different styles of writing the student accomplishes. For example, the pockets may be labeled First Drafts for all of the beginning writing a student does, Current Writing for the ongoing pages, and Finished Drafts for the final products. A fourth pocket might be labeled Writing Ideas for a list of topics for future writing and a fifth pocket might be labeled Personal for a student's reflections on any matters related to the unit. Sometimes, a teacher will ask the students to begin a list of the independently "published" classroom books the student has developed through the unit. Inside the back cover, a teacher can place a checklist of writing skills to indicate what each student has accomplished and maintained through the unit of study.

Peer Conferences

A peer-conference group is normally composed of five or six students who meet to assess the reports written by the group members related to the ITU. Each student takes a turn to tell the others what they need in the way of help, feedback, and ideas. The students hand their papers to their peers on the left and silently read the papers they receive. Each member writes his or her suggestions for improvement on duplicated response sheets, using phrases such as "Can you explain . . . ," "Can you tell more about . . . ," "I like . . . ," and "I thought this was interesting because. . . . " The response sheets are given to the appropriate authors of the reports so each student gets feedback from all of the other group members.

Teacher-Student Conferences and Conference Logs

A teacher-student conference is an arranged 10 to 15 minute meeting the teacher has with an individual student during the school day. The purpose is to help guide the student to self-assess his or her own educational progress, with a focus on the student's self-direction in learning. During the conference, one or two elements from the student's educational materials may be reviewed, including the log, various recordings, a writing folder, the daily journal, and so on. The atmosphere should remain friendly and helpful (i.e., nonjudgmental), and the student be encouraged to do most of the

In a peer conference, students hand their papers to peers on the left, who write suggestions for improvement on response sheets.

talking—focusing on any "downshifting" or other difficulties the student is having, discussing his or her feelings about the assignments, and telling about any social problems in the school environment that may be threatening or interrupting the student's learning progress.

A conference log is a notebook in which the teacher writes notes about each student's conference. It also contains a time schedule of meetings with the individual students. Using a sheet with the student's name and conference date on it, the teacher can record what was discussed and what elements from the student's educational materials were reviewed. For example, if a portion of the student's writing was discussed, the teacher could make notes about the student's work and, if mentioned by the student, what the next writing project would concern. Notes might also be made in the conference log about the student's invented spelling (if any) and about the teacher's suggestions related to grammar and structure for the student's final revision.

Debriefings for Specific Experiences

A debriefing for a specific experience is a "what we learned" type of discussion with the purpose of assessing a single event or happening, such as a field trip or visitor to the classroom or the culmination of an ITU. In a class meeting, the students usually summarize the things they thought were important and any new learning they acquired. The teacher often has students record their remarks on a chart, the writing board, or an overhead transparency. If a class meeting was held before the specific experience, in which students discussed what they wanted to learn through the experience, then the debriefing should focus on comparing what students anticipated learning with what they did learn.

B.   Assessment Criteria

For assessment in some situations, the teacher may want to use a clearly established set of criteria (i.e., a rubric in the sense that it is an established method or form) that identifies differences in the students' achievement. The set of criteria usually outlines ways for students to work toward mastery of identified learning objectives (outcomes). In this section, we review some of the criteria that educators have designed to assess student achievement.

Criteria for Student Problem Solving in Mathematics

The California Assessment Program (Stenmark, 1989) designed a rating system for problem solving in mathematics. The rating is from highest to lowest:

> *6*—exemplary response
>
> *5*—competent response
>
> *4*—minor errors but generally satisfactory
>
> *3*—serious errors but nearly satisfactory
>
> *2*—begins but fails to complete the task
>
> *1*—unable to begin effectively
>
> *0*—no attempt made

Criteria for Student Writing

The Texas Education Agency (1993) developed the following criteria for the scoring of student writing:

> *Score Point 4*—correct purpose, mode, audience; effective elaboration; consistent organization; clear sense of order and completeness; fluent
>
> *Score Point 3*—correct purpose, mode, audience; moderately well elaborated; organized but possible brief digressions; clear, effective language
>
> *Score Point 2*—correct purpose, mode, audience; some elaboration; some specific details; gaps in organization; limited language control
>
> *Score Point 1*—attempts to address audience; brief, vague, unelaborated; wanders off topic; lack of language control; little or no organization; wrong purpose and mode

More Criteria for Student Writing

The Manitoba Writing Assessment Program (Cooper and Odell, 1977) developed the following marking scale for the scoring of student writing:

> *Highly impressive*—the writing was well above average in thought, sentence structure, and word choice and was mostly free from errors
>
> *Commendable*—the writing showed command of thought, sentence structure, and word choice and was relatively free from error
>
> *Questionable*—the writing was only functional in terms of thought, sentence structure, and word choice, and the writer was in the need of instruction
>
> *Minimal*—the writing was in need of remediation and appeared to be on a frustration level
>
> *Insufficient material*—the writing was below minimal

Criteria for Specific Points in Writing

The Manitoba Writing Assessment Program (Cooper and Odell, 1977) also developed specific points for feedback. The specific points for the students' writing are:

> *4 points*—when the topic includes ideas that relate to the topic
>
> *3 points*—when the writing fluctuates but has a focus on the topic
>
> *2 points*—when the writing deviates from the topic
>
> *1 point*—when there is insufficient evidence related to the topic

Criteria for Student Use of Verbs

The Texas Education Agency (1993) developed the following criteria for the assessment of the use of specific verbs in writing. This example details the assessment:

> *4*—verbs are exact and exciting
>
> *3*—most verbs are interesting
>
> *2*—only a few verbs are vivid

1—very few verbs are interesting

0—no vivid verbs used

Criteria for Science Tasks

The Texas Education Agency (1993) also developed the following criteria to match science tasks (Barufaldi, Carnahan, and Rakow, 1991). For example, one science task is for a student to design an experiment when given this direction: "Describe the kind of tests you will do to find the answer." The criteria scoring for the student's response consists of the following:

3—the design allows for the comparison of variables and indicates the sufficient number of tests to obtain meaningful data

2—the design allows for the comparison of variables but lacks a sufficient number of tests to obtain meaningful data

1—the design allows for the comparison of the variable to the standard

0—fails to develop any type of plan

C.   General Guidelines for Assessment

Regardless of the approaches you choose to collect data about the students, you will be assessing what the students *write*, what the students *do*, and what the students *say*. Perhaps you will want to assess the students' skills and knowledge before the ITU is introduced. You might engage students in creating schema maps about what they know or questions maps about what they want to know about the unit topic. This is called pre-assessment or diagnostic evaluation. You will certainly want to assess what learning is occurring during the ITU, called formative evaluation, and what skills and knowledge have been acquired at the end of instruction, called summative evaluation. At the end of the unit, the students might create scheme maps about what they now know about the topic, or they could respond to the questions on their earlier question maps and compare the later maps with the earlier ones.

To begin reflecting upon how to assess what students write, do, and say, consider the following guidelines for assessing what a student writes (Kellough and Roberts, 1994):

1. Read everything that a student writes at your direction. If a task is important enough for the student to do and he or she does it at your direction, it is equally important that you give your professional attention to the product of the student's efforts.
2. Let the specific instructional objectives guide the learning, and make sure the objectives correlate with the assignments, work sheets, homework, and group work that is performed.
3. Provide positive written or verbal comments about the student's work.
   a. Explain to the student in writing or in a conference what is good about his or her written work.
   b. If further progress is needed, write about appropriate ways of completing the task.
   c. Reread every comment you write, putting yourself in the shoes of the student and his or her parent or guardian. How will they interpret your comment? Is this the interpretation you wanted?

d. Accentuate the positive when reading the students' personal journals, in which they are encouraged to write, think about their thinking, and record their creative thoughts. Writing in a personal journal gives a student practice in expressing his or her thoughts in written form, and that should be a nonthreatening situation. If the teacher makes a negative comment or evaluative statement, the student might be discouraged from recording creative and spontaneous expression in the journal. A better way is to talk individually with a student and ask for clarification. An effective teacher gains a great deal of insight into the student's thought processes and writing skills by reading and responding to the students' personal journal (a component of diagnostic evaluation).

e. Talk individually with each student about the progress in learning he or she is showing through the materials collected in the portfolio. Focus on the idea that the purpose of a portfolio is to allow the student to assess where he or she has been and what progress has been made to the present. The key word is *progress* in the student-teacher discussion.

Now turn your attention to the following guidelines for assessing what a student does and says. These guidelines will assist in evaluating the student's verbal and nonverbal behaviors in the academic environment:

1. Establish an anecdotal record for each student.
2. For a specific activity, list desirable behaviors and check the behaviors against the specific instructional objectives.
3. Make a record of your observations as quickly as possible. Perhaps you will be fortunate enough to be able to use audio or video recordings or a computer software program. If not, allot time to record your observations while they are still imprinted firmly in your memory—perhaps by selecting a specific time during the school day, or immediately after the class is dismissed for the day, or a time later in the evening.
4. Record your professional judgment about the student's progress toward a desired behavior. Also record comments that will serve as reminders to yourself about professional activities, such as "Check validity of observation by further testing" and "Discuss the observations with the school counselor."

Regardless of which assessment approaches you have chosen, you will need to evaluate what the students write, say, and do against the instructional objectives of the ITU. You might want to check an objective with more than one method and by more than one assessment checklist or other instrument. You might want to compare the results of one assessment technique against another to check for validity (the degree to which the assessment technique measures that which it is intended to measure) and thus try to reduce some of the subjectivity inherent in the assessment process. (Reliability is the accuracy with which an assessment technique consistently measures that which it does measure.)

D.   Examples of Assessment in an Integrated Curriculum

Assessment at a Junior High

Recently, at Natomas Junior High in Sacramento, California, a "school within a school"—also known as a Charter School with "extras"—was opened with the purpose of providing students and their parents with input and options in education. During each of the assessment periods, thematic units were developed to connect the various areas of curriculum to the California State Frameworks, which outlined concepts, goals, and skills instruction in language arts, science, math, social science, the visual and performing arts, and physical education (Warner, 1994). Knowledge and skills in various disciplines were integrated into themes that proved meaningful to the lives of the students and provided students with a deeper understanding of their culture. Life on a River, one such theme, had students writing poetry and reports about the Mississippi River and reading *Life on the Mississippi* by Mark Twain. The students also measured water currents (mathematics) and studied the ecology ecosystems (science) found along the river's length. In addition, they made drawings and sketches (art) of scenes along the Mississippi.

Parents Involved in Evaluation.   As part of the assessment of the school curriculum—which is over 60 percent exploratory in its structure—parents are required to be involved in the development of Differentiated Educational Plans for their children as well as in the learning activities, connections with the community, and work experience projects in which their children participate. The Differentiated Educational Plans are developed at the first of each school year by the students, their parents, and the staff of the school. The Charter School does not use letter grades. With the parents' input, goals are mutually agreed upon and a plan for achieving these goals is discussed. As the goals and plan are discussed, they are written by the teacher on school letterhead stationery. Then, the page of goals (a contract) is signed by the students, parents, and staff members, which serves to demonstrate their commitment to the plan. Each student's success is based on his or her effort toward the goals and any actual achievement of the goals during each assessment period. Developing their own Educational Plans seems to give students flexibility in learning and allows them to have options in meeting certain standards in learning.

Assessment Portfolios.   Since grades are not used, the students develop their own assessment portfolios, which are accumulating ones. Toward the end of each assessment period, for example, the students put together their own portfolios to show examples of their work. Other documents are included, too, such as the students' Differentiated Educational Plans, which reflect the behavioral and academic needs that were established at the beginning of the academic year. With the portfolios, the students can see ways they have achieved their personal goals and made positive contributions at school and in the community. As students "take charge" of their own learning, their self-esteem, self-worth, and enthusiasm for life and learning seem to increase.

Assessment at an Elementary School

In 1993 Bowling Green Elementary School in Sacramento, California, also became a Charter School and also embraced an integrated thematic instruction, an extended year-round calendar, and mastery of standards adopted by students, parents, and staff members (Mah, 1994). The parents helped set student performance standards and, on an ongoing basis, collected data to determine the extent to which the school's program was meeting those standards.

Difficulties in Assessment

As the descriptions of the two charter schools imply, assessment in such a school can be difficult for a teacher because it needs to be done in a way that is congruent with what is happening in the integrated curriculum. For example, if one of the purposes is for the students to be involved in their own learning, then the teacher will watch for behavior that would show the extent to which the students are truly involved, behaviors such as sharing with others, cooperating, and assuming responsibility. Sometimes, a teacher will note that the students are taking time to think through problems as they confront them. Perhaps the students will show that they are improving in their work products. At other times, a teacher will note to what extent the students are using the communicative tools of learning—reading, writing, and orally communicating—or are using certain conventions in spelling. The teacher will be aware that the students' progress must be noted in terms of where each student was prior to the introduction of an integrated curriculum. That is, a student's achievement must not be compared with another's or with national norms.

A Word about Report Cards

If a district requires that a teacher place letter grades on a student's report card instead of comments about the extent of the student's progress, the teacher may use the writing and reading samples that have been collected during the unit to support the letter grades the student has earned. During a conference with the student's parents or guardians, such samples can be reviewed. For additional documentation related to the comments written on cards, the teacher may want to include in the report card a checklist and narrative paragraphs.

E.   Assessing the Unit with Field Testing

Working Independently

You may be interested in assessing the ITU through field testing on your own. You can begin with the lessons you planned to teach to initiate the ITU. As the unit continues, consider the ITU from daily perspectives. Write down the successes and failures each day so you can make adjustments to your teaching along the way—part of your formative evaluation of the unit. Gather information about the students' progress in the unit in various ways, including informal observations, observations of student performance, and assessments of students' written work. Gather information that relates specifically to your learning objectives. You might consider developing an overall checklist about the information related to the unit for your assessment record. It can be a place for recording notes about a student's participation, behavior, and development of skills and knowledge. The sample list in Figure 4.1 might be similar to the one that a teacher develops for use in an ITU (see Planning Master 6).

Each day, you should consider what needs to be changed, how it could be changed, and how soon the changes can be made. After the ITU has been finished, you should write down what, if any, revisions you will make in the future—part of your summative evaluation of the unit.

Sample List for Assessment

Name of student _____   Date _____

Name of teacher _____   Time _____

1. Can identify theme, topic, main idea of the unit
2. Can identify contributions of others to the theme
3. Can identify problems related to the unit study
4. Has developed skills in:

Application of information	_____
Classifying	_____
Categorizing	_____
Decision-making	_____
Discussion	_____
Gathering resources	_____
Justification of choices	_____
Location of information	_____
Organization of information	_____
Reading text	_____
Reading maps and globes	_____
Reporting to others	_____
Self-evaluation	_____
Study habits	_____
Summary preparation	_____
Working with others	_____
Working independently	_____
Other features unique to the unit	_____

Additional teacher comments:

Figure 4.1   Sample Assessment List

Working with Team Members

On an agreed-upon date, team members should present the lesson(s) each has agreed to teach. As the unit continues, the team can field test the ITU in various ways. Perhaps members could trade classes, or members could participate in some team teaching. For instance, two members could combine their classes for instruction in the ITU—if this is possible within the school's scheduling arrangements.

During a common planning period (and periodically if needed), members should meet as a group in order to assess the progress of the ITU. This is where you will want to discuss recent successes and failures in the lessons—part of the team's ongoing formative evaluation of the unit. Together, team members can brainstorm what needs to be changed in the ITU, how the unit could be changed, and when such changes could be done. After the ITU has been finished, the team should meet again to discuss what revisions in the ITU should be made for future use—part of the team's summative evaluation of the unit.

Summary

In this chapter, we presented various assessment techniques that will be useful in discovering what your students are learning (assessment) and in comparing what they are learning with what you want them to be learning as stated in your objectives (evaluation). We pointed out that much of the student assessment needs to be done in an informal way and as a continuous process. The teacher needs to observe the students and make judgments about the quality and quantity of their work. The teacher's observations and informal methods of assessment are central to the evaluation of learning, and the teacher will want to keep carefully annotated records for each student so the progress of learning is reported accurately. Several assessment techniques—anecdotal records, audio and video recordings, checklists, diaries, and portfolios—were discussed. The exercises were designed so you could explore the use of portfolios in assessment and develop a checklist for assessment in your own classroom.

Chapter Notes

1. Kentucky now requires that all high school seniors produce writing portfolios. For an informative discussion of how one high school teacher has combined portfolios and innovative writing assignments in the classroom, see Elizabeth Everett, "Do the Write Thing," *The Science Teacher* 61, 7 (October, 1994): 35–7.
2. Assistance in the use of portfolios for assessment can be found in *Portfolios News*, a bulletin published by the Portfolio Assessment Clearinghouse. Write to San Diequito High School District, 710 Encinitas Blvd., Encinitas, CA, 02024.

Questions and Activities for Discussion

1. Despite your best intentions, is it possible that there will be some students who fail to construct meaning in what they do? In what ways might this be determined in the classroom? How might it be remedied? Participate in a discussion of examples put forth by group members.
2. One criticism about the importance of content in teaching with ITUs is related to the necessary connection of content to books from the library or from home. For example, suppose the students in your classroom have been reading a library book and an extension activity is presented in which the children study the geographic area that is the setting in the book. The geographic area is the same, or similar to, the area in which the children live. In your opinion, should the students study whatever happens to appear in a book that they read (or the teachers read to them)? Must what is read have to be related to the content mandated by school curriculum documents? Should the students only be introduced to the content mandated by school, district, and state documents? What resources would help you determine the content in children's books that relates to content required by your school? In what other ways can you ensure that your students are being introduced to required content?
3. Some critics have mentioned that different disciplines should be dealt with differently in ITUs because all disciplines are not equivalent in importance and value. In your opinion, are all disciplines equivalent? Why or why not? What helped you form your opinion? In what ways could you determine which disciplines to include or not to include in an ITU?

Chapter

5

Examining Thematic Units

The important thing is not to stop questioning.

—*Albert Einstein*

PROBLEM SOLVING AND DECISION MAKING IN THE REAL WORLD IS AN INTEGRATED ACTIVITY

On any given day or specified time period, teacher and students can look at a problem or subject of study from the point of view of many separate disciplines. Such an integrated approach to some matter of concern has been adopted not only by educators but by other professionals as well. For example, consider the fact-finding and decision-making approach of public officials in Colorado when confronted with the task of making decisions about projects proposed for watersheds in their state. While gathering information, the officials brought in Dave Rosgen, a state hydrologist. Rosgen led the officials into the field to demonstrate specific ways by which he helped control erosion and rehabilitate damaged streams. He took the officials to Wolf Creek, where they donned high waders. Rosgen led the group down the creek to examine various features of that complex natural stream. He pointed out evidence of the creek's past meanders, patterns that he had incorporated into his rehabilitation projects (Little, 1992). In addition to listening to this scientist's point of view, the officials listened to other experts to consider related economic and political issues, for example, before making final decisions about projects that had been proposed for watersheds in that state.

During interdisciplinary thematic units, the students will study a topic and its underlying ideas as well as related knowledge from various disciplines on an ongoing basis. The teacher, sometimes with the help of the students and other teachers and adults, will introduce experiences designed to foster ideas and skills from various disciplines, just as Rosgen introduced information from hydrology to develop reading and language arts skills through the unit. For instance, the teacher might stimulate communication skills through creative writing and other projects. Throughout the unit, the teacher guides the students in exploring ideas related to different disciplines.

● ●

I n Chapter 4 we focused attention on various assessment techniques developed to enable you and your students to discover their progress in learning, generally by comparing what they are learning or did learn with what they were expected to learn. We mentioned that the students' personal inquiries were central to an ITU and that much of the student assessment needed to be done both informally and continuously. We discussed the value of assessing the status of individual students and groups. Several assessment techniques—anecdotal records, recordings, checklists, portfolios, and others—were reviewed to assist you in establishing accurate records and reports.

In this chapter we present some examples about teaching today's students effectively through an integrated curriculum rather than by teaching each subject of the curriculum as a separate and unrelated entity. You will see the ways that different teachers have planned their thematic units for different grade levels.

For both your study and potential use, we present three detailed examples of interdisciplinary thematic units:

1. *Ancient Greece.* For use in middle and secondary grades; divided into eleven lessons.
2. *Early Explorers and Settlers in North America.* Adaptable for use in middle and secondary grades; divided into six lessons.
3. *Spring.* For use in primary grades (specifically for kindergarten and first grade); divided into five lessons.

As you study these three ITUs, pay special attention to the margin notes, the three types of which are related to:

- management (M)
- technology and teaching aids such as media, children's literature, and learning center kits (T)
- diversity (D)

Sample ITU 1: Ancient Greece—The Dawn of a New Age

Middle and Secondary Grades.   The unit revolves around several disciplines, including geography, science, social science, mathematics, physical education, and literature. It was developed to help students learn about ancient Greece and to make comparisons between life today and life 2000 years ago in Greece. As presented here, the unit could be taught by one teacher or, with some slight modifications, by a team of teachers.

> **D** Activities should be varied and represent a holistic approach to the topic.

Unit Overview

This ITU includes a wide variety of multisensory activities involving language arts, mathematics, science, art, drama, social studies, health, and physical education. Each lesson requires 45 to 75 minutes, with Lessons 1 and 11 each requiring two consecutive days. This unit will take about three weeks. In addition to the eleven detailed lesson plans, there are several extension activities.

This unit was planned for a class of thirty-four students, though it would be suitable for a class of any size. Since most classrooms contain students with diverse abilities and backgrounds, the unit was designed with such students in mind. Only minor accommodations will be necessary for students with special needs. The unit was originally designed for grades 5–9, but it is adaptable for any grade 5–12.

The unit contains several cooperative learning activities that assume students have had prior experience working in cooperative groups. If students have not had such prior experience, these lessons should be preceded by a discussion of the expected behaviors and responsibilities when working cooperatively with others. It is recommended that students be in teams of three or four at the start of the unit, because this will facilitate an easy transition into group work and allow for a team-based behavior management system, if so desired.

To support this unit, an arranged environment should be created in the classroom (or classrooms). This supportive environment might include posters, artifacts, Greek music, trade and resource books, and simple toga costumes that can be worn during specific activities. Bulletin boards could be created utilizing the students' myths from Lesson 4 as well as the vase art extension activity.

> **M** The actual time length of each lesson and number of class periods will depend on the intellectual level of your students and the nature of the scheduling at your school. Many of the activities will consume full class periods. A teacher can incorporate any of the ideas in the margin notes for facilitating cooperative group activities or instituting the technology ideas.

General Goals

This unit is designed to explore

- The major changes in Greek society from 2000 to 400 B.C.
- Greek mythology
- The effects of Greece's geography on its people and their way of life

---

Source: Unpublished work by Nancy Mortham. Reprinted by permission.

- How the early Olympic Games differ from those held today
- The class structure in early Athenian society
- Greek architecture
- Two very different city-states: Sparta and Athens

This unit was designed to incorporate these goals of the California History/Social Studies Framework:

- Knowledge and Cultural Understanding
- Democratic Understanding and Civic Values
- Skills Attainment and Social Participation

M Class meetings can help establish class expectations, matters of misbehavior, and consequences (Glasser, 1986).

Assessment

There are three components for student assessment of learning: (1) the students' unit folders, (2) the unit test, and (3) anecdotal notes. Additionally, students are encouraged to assess their own performances through self-assessment and group assessments.

. . . .
LESSON 1
. . . .

Introduction to Ancient Greece

Objective

After reading the assigned text material and utilizing resource books and posters around the room, students will create small group presentations, which will be performed for the class.

Materials

Resource books, posters, artifacts, student text.

Anticipatory Set

"Today we are beginning an exciting unit on ancient Greece. We will participate in a wide variety of activities and have many opportunities to work in cooperative groups on special presentations and projects." Assess prior student knowledge by eliciting what they know about ancient Greece. Write their responses in a list. Then, with students, review the list in order to group similar entries, such as those related to clothing, shelter, activities, and so on. Let students "reserve" topics for personal inquiry. "Today we are going to form groups that will be in place for the remainder of the unit."

D The more diverse the students, the greater the need for an integrated curriculum and active learning with partners (Garcia, 1994).

Procedure

1. Put students in teams of four or five students per team.
2. Assign each team a topic to research from one of the following:
   The Minoan Age
   The Myceanaean Age
   The First Olympics
   The Age of Expansion
   The First Use of Coins

D Higher-level high school students could research and present the most salient points of each time period.

3. Student teams create presentations to be performed in front of the class the next day or later, depending on the grade level, the complexity of their presentations, and the research needed. This may be done in the form of a play, newscast, report, discussion, and so forth.
4. The following day (or a later day), students present to the class.

M Task outcomes should be clearly specified for students (Tikunoff, 1983).

5. After each presentation, team members prepare an outline on the board to include who, what, when, where, and why or how.

6. The presenters respond to questions as the class takes notes on the information presented.

7. After the presentations, the students evaluate their own listening behavior.

Closure

"What is something interesting that you learned today and that you didn't know before? Did your group have any problems while researching information or putting together your presentations?" Discuss cooperation when working in groups and the importance of giving each member of the group a chance to contribute ideas.

Evaluation

Group presentations are teacher evaluated according to content. Students self-assess their listening behavior using the assigned evaluation form.

T   Video: *Conversations with Ancient Greeks* (Cinema Guild, 1992), grades 9 and above. Brings Socrates, Odysseus, Euripedes, and other figures from ancient history into the present as the figures share their ideas in a conversational setting. They tell how their contributions affected the present. Includes breaks for student discussions.

T   Video: *Effective Listening Skills: Listening to What You Hear* (Cambridge Career Prods., 1992), grades 7–12. Delivers information about the acronym DRIVE and the related listening skills for which the letters stand— Deciding to listen, Reading all stimuli, Investing time wisely, Verifying what was heard, and Expending energy to listen.

M   Ginott (1971) suggests that teachers model the expected behavior and that messages be sent to students that acknowledge students' feelings, invite cooperation, give appropriate directions, and express feelings about a situation rather than a student's character.

•••••••••••••••••••••••••••••••••••••

LESSON 2

•••••••••••••••••••••••••••••••••••••

Time Lines

Objective

After a review of the major events of early Greek history and the development of a sample time line, students will draw their own time lines documenting significant events of this period.

Materials

Text as a resource; white, unlined paper; rulers; masking tape time line on the classroom floor.

Anticipatory Set

"Yesterday, your groups presented information based on what was read about different events in early Greece. Today we are going to create a time line so that we can see the progression of events over time as they occurred in Greece."

Procedure

1. Discuss the purpose of the time line, how to read it, and the meaning of B.C. and A.D.
2. Create a sample time line on the board using important personal dates offered by members of the class.
3. Point out the masking tape time line on the floor, and ask each group to select one person to stand at the correct spot on the time line that represents the event or period they presented yesterday, thus creating a "people time line."
4. After students are in place, they give a brief review of the information they presented yesterday. Stress the very long span of time in comparison to the history of the United States.
5. Students create their own time lines on paper, which include all of the dates represented by the students on the "people time line." These time lines, then, include dates for the Minoan Age, the Myceanaean Age, the first Olympics, and so on.

M Students should primarily be instructed in small groups, and academically related discourse should be encouraged. There can be assigned academic tasks with intermittent teacher assistance.

D Use the strategies indicated within the lesson procedures to provide additional opportunities to expand the study within each lesson to meet individual student or class needs.

T Computer Software: *Student Writing Center for Windows* (The Learning Center, 1993), grades 5–12. Operating system: MS-DOS and Windows 3.1. This has a word-processing and publishing program for student reports, newsletters, letters, and journals.

Closure

"We have been talking about events in Greece dating back to 2000 B.C. Raise your hand if you can tell me how many years ago that was. If a time line was written the same way as the number lines we see in math, how would we write the numbers that we refer to as B.C.?" Those numbers would be negative numbers.

Evaluation

Observe students as they form the "people time line" and as they create their own timelines with the given information.

LESSON 3

Vocabulary

Objective

After completing a vocabulary scribble, students will define and illustrate the vocabulary words.

Materials

Vocabulary scribble; textbook as resource.

Anticipatory Set

"Early Greeks stored grain in large vases, and examples of these are displayed around the room. Today you are going to color code a vase based on the vocabulary from our Greece unit."

D Vocabulary words for this activity will vary depending on the grade level, English language skills, and intellectual maturity of the students.

Procedure

1. Describe how the students may color code the vase (Figure 5.1) (the word and its definition must be colored the same color). Students may suggest other ways to match words with definitions.
2. Students should use the text as a resource.
3. Allow students time to complete the activity (about 15 min.).
4. As students complete their scribble, they may begin writing definitions and creating illustrations for each word. After beginning in class under the teacher's guidance, this activity should be completed as homework.

Word List

barter	democracy	tragedy
comedy	monarchy	sanctuary
helot	oligarchy	city-state
ephor	tyrant	

Closure

"Which of these words define a form of government? Which of these words are nouns that describe a person in ancient Greece? Two of the words are still used today to describe plays and other entertainment. Which are they?"

D The "coloring" activity asks students to complete a higher-level task—to match terms and their definitions. This activity both supports a need for LEP students and sequences appropriate conceptual growth in building knowledge about ancient Greece.

Evaluation

The vocabulary scribble and the definitions and illustrations are included in each student's Greece folder.

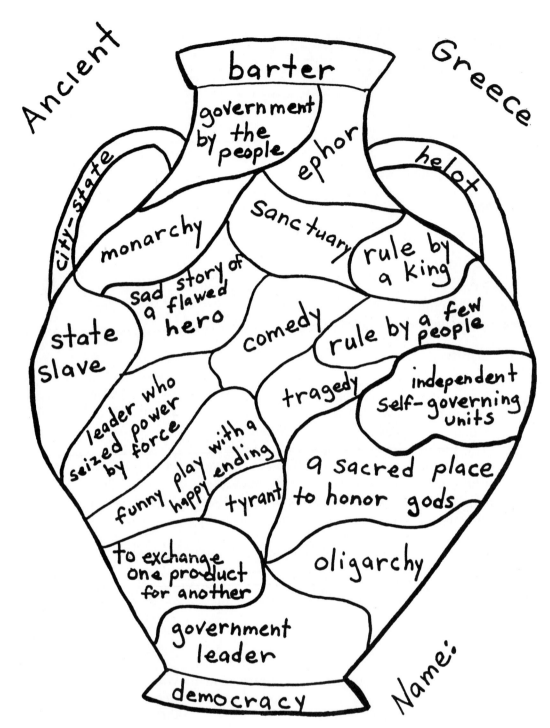

Figure 5.1 Vocabulary Scribble

```
• • • • • • • • • • • • • • • • • • • • • • • • • • • • • • •
```
LESSON 4
```
• • • • • • • • • • • • • • • • • • • • • • • • • • • • • • •
```

Greek Myths

Objective

After listening to and reading Greek myths and discussing what constitutes a myth, students will write their own myths.

Materials

Prometheus and the Story of Fire by I. M. Richardson (New Jersey, Troll Associates, 1983); overhead transparency of "Perseus Meets the Medusa" (adapted by Lanette Whitnell from *D'Aulaires' Book of Greek Myths*); visual display that illustrates the components of a myth.

Anticipatory Set

"I'd like to share with you a poster that will help you remember the major components of a myth." Present and discuss the poster depicting a large black cauldron, entitled Brew Up a Myth. On the cauldron are cards that read Imagination, Mystery, Pre-Science Explanation of Nature, and Belief in Supernatural Powers.

Procedure

1. Teacher reads aloud *Prometheus and the Story of Fire*.
2. While brainstorming, students compare/contrast myths and legends. Teacher records student ideas on the board and then encourages students to add to the descriptions on the myth cauldron.
3. Students participate in a choral reading of "Perseus Meets the Medusa."
4. Students write their own myths.

Closure

"Raise your hand if you think you can explain why the stories we heard and read today are classified as myths rather than as legends." Students may refer to the myth poster for assistance.

T Activity center: *Greek Mythology* (Tapes 'n Books for Gifted Education, 314–350 Weinacker Ave., P.O. Box 6448, Mobile, AL 3660), grades 5–12. Includes task cards with activities keyed to Bloom's taxonomy, with an emphasis on student tasks related to classification of the cognitive domain.

D More advanced literature can be substituted according to students' reading level.

M It is important to communicate to students that you know what is occurring in the classroom through nonverbal interactions (handshakes, smiles), as well as to emphasize rules, rewards, and consequences with the understanding that the responsibility for good behavior rests with each student individually (Skinner, 1968).

Evaluation

After students complete their rough drafts, they receive feedback from their peers using the Myth Checklist as a guide (Figure 5.2). Final drafts are teacher evaluated using this established rubric:

The myth demonstrates a belief in higher powers (gods) 12.5 points
The myth explains something in nature   12.5 points
Writing skill   75.0 points

Evaluation of the writing skill considers purpose, mode, audience, effective elaboration, consistent organization, clear sense of order and completeness, and fluent and effective language (see criteria from Texas Education Agency, 1993, in Chapter 4 of this book.)

M The teacher should strive to promote cooperative group work and to provide adequate support for students' evaluations of one another's work.

Myth Checklist

1. Does this myth demonstrate a belief in higher powers (gods)?   yes   no

2. Does this myth try to explain something in nature?   yes   no

3. In this myth I like

4. Suggestions:

Author of the myth:

Peer reviewer:

Figure 5.2   Myth Checklist Used in Peer Evaluation

LESSON 5

Mapping

Objective

After creating a physical map of Greece and discussing how geography played an important role in the development of Greek society, students will complete information retrieval charts.

Materials

One map per cooperative learning group (CLG); papier mâché; glue; retrieval charts.

Anticipatory Set

"Today, in your cooperative learning groups, you are going to make a physical map of Greece. Each of you can contribute. When the map is complete, place it on the display table. Show the location of city-states on the map."

Procedure

1. Groups complete their maps.
2. In groups, students read the section of the text that deals with the geography of Greece.
3. As a class, students brainstorm how the geography affected
   a. farming (only a quarter of the land was suitable for growing grain; Greeks also grew grapes and olives)
   b. development of city-states (isolated, close-knit communities developed because of mountains and sea)
   c. trade (they traded by sea for goods they could not grow or make)
   d. culture (trade led to extensive contact with people from other cultures, which led to the spread of products and ideas)
4. Students complete their individual retrieval charts (Figure 5.3).

Closure

"Let's share some of our ideas from the retrieval charts." Students volunteer to share their responses. "Although both the geographic terrain and climate affect a culture, it takes people working together to build a community. The people who successfully settled in the Aegean region formed tightly knit communities to build and shape their civilization."

Evaluation

The geography retrieval charts are added to the Greece folder. Students' responses are evaluated during the discussion.

D   Rather than creating a physical map, the teacher may prefer to have students draw individual maps of Greece.

T   CD-ROM: *Geopedia* (Encyclopedia Britannica Ed. Corp., 1993), grades 5–8. This program has references, resources, and student activities (brain teasers) about Greece and other countries, regions, and cities of the world. Includes excellent photographs and video clips. Video: *Europe: Southern Region* (EBED, 1994), grades 6–12. This is an overview of Greece and southern Europe and the effects of the Mediterranean Sea on the climate of the region.

D   This lesson would complement science. Students could make connections of geographic location and climate which also would affect suitability for farming.

Ancient Greece Retrieval Chart

How did geography and climate influence ancient Greece in the following areas?

Farming:

Development of city-states:

Trade:

Culture:

Use the space below to record any important ideas you discover during this discussion.

Figure 5.3   Retrieval Chart to Be Completed by Students

LESSON 6

The Olympic Games

Objective

After comparing and contrasting the early Olympic Games with present day and watching a video of Olympic heroes from the past, students will brainstorm what qualities are important in an Olympic athlete.

Materials

Video: *The Olympic Challenge*.

Anticipatory Set

"What did you see in the video about the personal qualities of the athletes? Raise your hand if you can tell me something about the attitudes of the athletes you watched."

M Using think-pair-share, students could brainstorm their perceptions of the personal qualities of Olympic athletes as an anticipatory set.

Procedure

1. Discuss with students these aspects of the ancient Olympic Games:
   a. The purpose was to honor the gods.
   b. War ceased while the games were played.
   c. Only men participated.
   d. Games were held every four years.
   e. The Olympics began with just a 200-yard foot race and later included other races, boxing, wrestling, discus throw, horse racing, and chariot races.

2. Write the following question on the board, which students are to think about as they view the video: What personal qualities are often found in Olympic athletes?
3. Students view the video.
4. Make a list on the board as students share the qualities that make an Olympic athlete (e.g., perseverance, talent, pride, dedication, determination, courage, endurance).

M Procedures can be based on teacher lecture or student research/text reading.

Closure

"Many of the qualities that make a successful Olympic athlete are also the qualities of any successful person. What do you think this means?" Discuss goal setting, dreams, and so on.

Evaluation

The quantity of student contributions and the level of student thinking are recorded and or evaluated during class discussions.

•••••••••••••••••••••••••••••••••

LESSON 7

•••••••••••••••••••••••••••••••••

Discus Throwing Records

Objective

After observing the teacher create a bar graph on the board, students will design a bar graph that graphically displays given Olympic discus records.

Materials

Graph paper; overhead transparency; list of Olympic records.

Anticipatory Set

"Let's take a vote to find out which fruit is the favorite of most class members. Raise your hands if apples are your favorite. Oranges? Bananas?" Teacher writes information on the board and then creates a bar graph to display the results, thinking aloud while creating the graph. "The neat thing about a bar graph is that we don't have to look at the actual numbers to know at a glance which fruit is the favorite. We need only to compare heights on the bar graph."

Procedure

1. Students work individually to create a bar graph of Olympic discus records, given these figures:

Year	Distance in Feet
1896	96
1912	148
1932	162
1956	185
1972	211
1988	226
1996	?

2. Students make a prediction for the next summer Olympic Games based on previous years and then graph their prediction.
3. Students write a short paragraph explaining the reasons for their predictions.
4. Students discuss if they would like to make further predictions by collecting data and making more bar graphs.

M Management suggestions by Kounin (1970) include recognizing the effect of a teacher's response to one student's misbehavior on students whose behavior is appropriate, as well as the ability to be alert in class and to redirect potential student misbehavior.

Closure

"When we create and read bar graphs, we are more interested in making comparisons and observing for trends than in knowing the exact numbers that are graphed. How do the previous discus records help us in predicting what will happen in next summer's games?" Because the number of years between each discus record fluctuates, students must make their predictions by taking into account that there is only a difference of eight years from the 1988 entry to the 1996 Olympics. "What else would you like to predict on the basis of your collection of data and the creation of a bar graph?"

Evaluation

The bar graphs are included in each student's Greece folder. They also respond to the following open-ended question: Can these discus records continue to increase indefinitely?

D Make students accountable for researching Olympic records and creating bar graphs; girls might want to track women's records, for example. Evaluation could extend to performance assessment of students' creating bar graphs.

•••••••••••••••••••••••••••••••••
LESSON 8
•••••••••••••••••••••••••••••••••

Let the Games Begin

Objective

After discussing proper exercise procedures, computing target aerobic heart rates, and creating pulse-rate graphs, students will monitor and record their pulse rates while participating in movement activities.

Materials

16 Frisbees; straws; participation awards; graph paper; Target Heart Rate bulletin board; watch with second hand; blue,red,green crayons.

Anticipatory Set

"When is the last time you participated in a physical activity for at least fifteen minutes that made your heart beat faster and your body sweat? Today we are going to learn how to exercise safely and effectively so that we can be physically fit."

Procedure

1. Students brainstorm why it is important to exercise regularly.
2. Introduce the physical activity sequence: warm-up, stretch, aerobic activity, cool down.
3. Explain how maximum heart rates and target heart rates are calculated: maximum rate = 220 – age; target heart rate = 60–80% of maximum rate.
4. Students calculate their target heart rates, and then the teacher introduces the Target Heart Rate bulletin board (Figure 5.4).
5. Students create line graphs (Figure 5.4) to record the following color coded data:
     Resting pulse rate (in blue)
     Aerobic pulse rate (in red)
     Recovery pulse rate (in green)
6. Teach students proper procedure for taking and recording a 10-second pulse and record resting pulse rates.
7. Students participate in the following activities:
   warm up—fast walk around 0.1 of a mile course
   stretch—legs, arms, back
   aerobic—modified kickball, in which one entire team runs the bases while the outfield passes the ball and runs to form a circle at a designated place.

M Effective teachers specify task outcomes, have high expectations for students, and use active teaching behaviors (Garcia, 1994).

Figure 5.4   Target Heart Rate
Bulletin Board Display

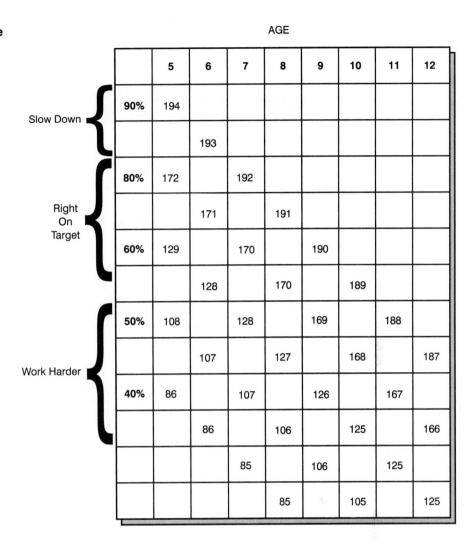

AGE

Slow Down

Right On Target

Work Harder

8. During activity, students take their aerobic pulse rates.
9. After a cool-down walk of several minutes, students take their recovery pulse rates.
10. Both pulse rates are recorded on students' graphs (Figure 5.5).
11. Students participate in a fun Olympic activity as a tie-in to the Ancient Greece unit:
    Javelin throw using straws
    Discuss throw using Frisbees

Closure

"Raise your hands if you can tell me the proper sequence of physical activity. Why is it important to warm up and stretch before an aerobic activity? Who can explain how we calculate our target heart rates? We will be keeping track of our pulse rates for the rest of this month as we participate in physical education activities. As you begin to exercise regularly, you will find that your resting pulse rate will become lower and your recovery rate will be quicker."

Evaluation

Pulse-rate graphs are added to each student's Ancient Greece folder. Students are encouraged to monitor their own improvement. Only those students who participate in the movement activities receive an award for participation, which is worth points at the end of the unit (Figure 5.6).

M Teachers have professional rights in their classrooms and can expect appropriate student behavior; students have the right to choose how to behave. The consequences for misbehavior should be stated clearly and firmly (Hill, 1990).

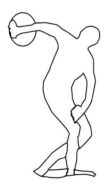

Ancient Greece

Games Day

Participation Award

Figure 5.6   Sample Participation Award

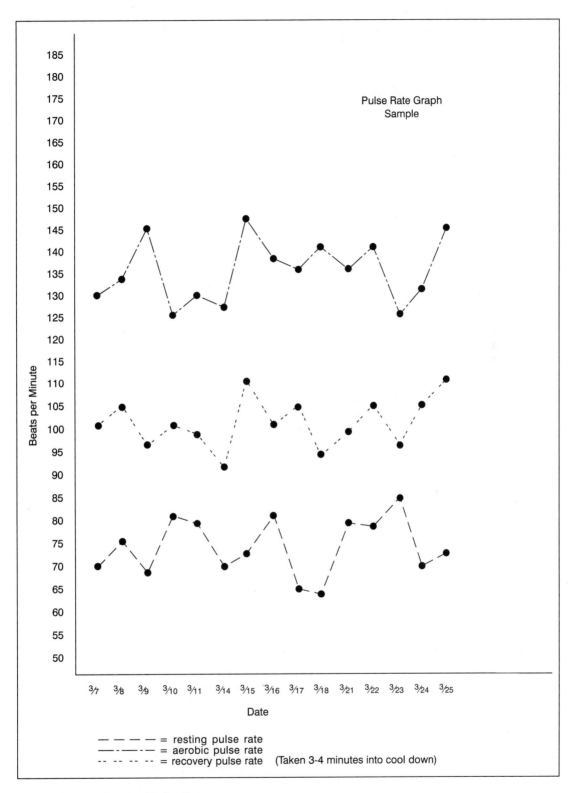

Figure 5.5 A Sample Graph of Pulse Rates

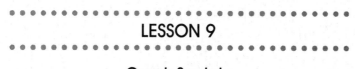

LESSON 9

Greek Society

Objective

After discussing the four classes of Athenian society, students will participate in a simulated town meeting and will complete their retrieval charts.

Materials

Retrieval charts; role-play description sheet; game cards for Citizen, Family of Citizen, Metic, Slave; identification necklaces for children, accused slave, accusing metic, and wife of citizen.

Anticipatory Set

As students enter the room, hand each student a game card, which will identify his or her role in the simulation. Explain briefly that they will be participating in a role-play and that they are to stay in character until the town meeting is finished. (Note: for a class of thirty-four, cards should be divided proportionately as follows: 15% citizens = five; 48% family of citizens = sixteen; 12% metics = four; and, 25% slaves = eight.)

Procedure

1. Arrange the classroom for a town meeting.
2. Discuss the four levels of Ancient Greek society:
   Citizens. Men over eighteen. They may vote, hold office, speak at town meetings, and own slaves, and they are protected by laws.
   Family members of citizens. Wives and children. They may not vote or speak at town meetings and have no rights, privileges or protection under law.
   Metics. Foreigners, tradesmen, shopkeepers, and craftsmen. They may not vote, nor hold office, but they may speak at town meetings and are protected under law.
   Slaves. Prisoners of wars and other captives. They may not vote or hold office. They have no protection under the law and no job choice, though they may have a family only with their master's permission.

3. Students read the scenario from the role-play description sheet (Figure 5.7).
4. Reiterate the roles and powers.
5. Students hold the town meeting.
6. Students form groups of three or four to complete the information retrieval chart (Figure 5.8).

Closure

"How would you differentiate among the roles of citizens, family members of citizens, metics, and slaves? Which would you prefer to be? How would you compare and contrast the democracy of Ancient Greece with democracy in the United States?"

Evaluation

The retrieval chart is a required element for the student folder. Students will also be assessed according to participation in the simulation.

Setup.
Eight chairs should be placed in the front of the room for the key characters in this simulated town meeting: five citizens, one metic, one wife of citizen, and one slave. Other chairs should be arranged in rows for those members of the town not allowed to speak in the meeting. Other metics should sit closest to the key characters in case they wish to speak.

Scenario.
While at the busy town center where metics were selling their wares earlier in the day, turmoil erupted. A slave who was accompanying the family members of a citizen was accused of stealing food from one of the metics. The only ones actually saw this happen was the metic, who accuses the slave of stealing, and the wife of the slave owner, who claims it was not the slave but another thief who is at fault. Since slaves have no legal rights and are not citizens, a crime such as stealing can result in severe fines for the slave owner and possible banishment or even death for the accused slave.

The slave owner is called to a town meeting and he is accompanied by the rest of his family. All other citizens and people of the town are present at this meeting. They listen to arguments both from the metic's point of view and from the slave owner's point of view. The slave owner's wife quietly supplies her husband with information but is not allowed to speak to the assembly. The accused slave is not allowed to speak. The slave owner, since he is a citizen, is the only one who can speak on behalf of the slave. The metics may speak, but they cannot vote as to the guilt or innocence of the accused slave.

After all arguments have been heard, the citizens take a vote to determine the verdict.

Figure 5.7 Role-Play Description Sheet

Greek Society

Level	Description	Rights	Responsibilities
Citizens			
Family of Citizens			
Metics			
Slaves			

Compare democracy in United States today with the democracy of ancient Greek society. List the similarities and differences.

Similarities	Differences

Figure 5.8 Information Retrieval Chart

• •

LESSON 10

• •

Column Experiment

Objective

After discussing ancient Greek architecture and the scientific method, students will experiment to discover which of the given column designs will support the most weight.

Materials

Data collection form; 9 × 12 inch construction paper; tape; rulers; supplemental teaching information form; pictures illustrating the three architectural styles.

Anticipatory Set

"Let's take a minute to look around the room at the pictures of ancient Greece that show us examples of their architecture. Raise your hand if you think you can tell me something about how the early Greeks built structures."

Procedures

1. Encourage students to share what they already know or think they know about architectural design.
2. Using the supplemental teaching information (Figure 5.9) as a resource, discuss the three orders of Greek architecture: Doric, Ionic, and Corinthian. Show examples of each.
3. Discuss the steps of the scientific method and why it should be thought of as a cyclic rather than a linear process (i.e., as new data come in, an earlier conclusion may be thrown out, and the process repeats all over again).
4. Describe the experiment the students will conduct and clarify any questions they may have about it. Then give students the instructions for the column experiment (Figure 5.10).
5. Put students in their cooperative learning groups and assign the following roles: recorder, runner, gatekeeper, thinker.
6. Allow students enough time to conduct their testing and to record their results.

Classical Greek Architecture

General Information

The earliest buildings of Greece were made of sun-dried bricks, timber and decorative terra-cotta. Later, stone and marble became the chief materials. Mortar was rarely used, the finely cut blocks being held by metal dowels and clamps. Although Greek architects were aware of the arch and vault, their approach was relatively conservative. The megaron, with its portico entrance and low-pitched roof, was the model for Greek temples. The earliest temples were timber; their forms were later translated into mud-brick and finally, stone. The two basic elements of timber structures, vertical supports (columns) and horizontal members (entablatures), were transformed into the three carefully proportioned orders, or styles, of Greek architecture: the Doric, Ionic, and Corinthian.

The Doric: The earliest and simplest of the classical orders. The fluted columns stand firmly on their platform without intermediate bases. The abacus is deep and plain.

The Ionic: This elegant order is recognized by the capital (head of the column) of spiral-shaped scrolls called *volutes*.

The Corinthian: The last and most elaborate order. The tall fluted column was capped by an elaborate stylized carving of acanthus plants. The decorative character of this order made it popular

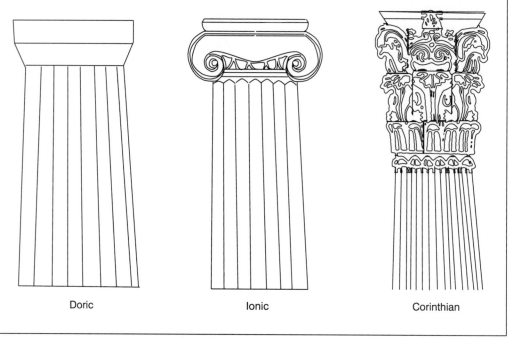

| Doric | Ionic | Corinthian |

Figure 5.9 Supplemental Teaching Information Sheet
Source: Adapted from *The Book of Buildings: A Traveler's Guide* by Richard Reid (Michael Joseph Limited, 1980).

Column Experiment

Focus question: Will a single sheet of paper support a heavy book? Try this experiment to find out.

Purpose: What do I want to find out?
Which of the tested columns will support the most weight?

Hypothesis: What do I think?

Experiment:
1. Roll a 9" x 12" piece of construction paper so that it is 9 inches long and has a diameter of 1 inch.
2. Stand the paper on end to form a 9-inch high column.
3. Add math books to the column until the column collapses.
4. Repeat with the following column specifications: 9 inches long with a 2-inch diameter; 6 inches long (folded in half) with a 1-inch diameter; and 6 inches long (folded in half) with a 2-inch diameter.

Analysis: Collect and interpret data

Relative Strengths of Various Columns

Number of math books

12					
11					
10					
9					
8					
7					
6					
5					
4					
3					
2					
1					
0					
	9 x 1	9 x 2	6 x 1 (doubled)	6 x 2 (doubled)	

Conclusions: What did I learn?

What questions do I now have? (This will lead to a new purpose, perhaps a new experiment)

Figure 5.10   Instructions for the Column Experiment

Closure

Ask groups to share their results and then write those results on the board. Discuss the need to make multiple trial tests when conducting an experiment. Have students calculate the average result for each tested column using the data collected from the board.

Evaluation

The completed experiment forms are included in each student's Greece folder. Each student's level of understanding is assessed by reviewing the student's conclusions and by further questioning.

● ●

LESSON 11

● ●

Sparta/Athens

Objective

After discussing selected terms, students will research an assigned topic and report on it to the class.

Materials

Text; resources already available in classroom.

Anticipatory Set

"When we discussed the geography of Greece, we talked about the development of city-states. What is a city-state? Are there any in existence today?" Singapore is a modern city-state. "Which city would have been a better place to live, Athens or Sparta?"

Procedures

1. Discuss these terms: *government, economy, lifestyle, monarchy, oligarchy,* and *democracy*. For background, use the teacher information sheet (Figure 5.11).
2. Have students count off by eight, creating eight random groups of four students each (in a class of thirty-two).
3. Assign the following topics, one to each of the eight groups.

Government/Athens	Government/Sparta
Education/Athens	Education/Sparta
Economy/Athens	Economy/Sparta
Lifestyle/Athens	Lifestyle/Sparta

4. Student teams research their topics.
5. Groups present their information to the class and create an outline on the board. The focus should be on comparing and contrasting Athens and Sparta.
6. Students ask questions of the presenters and take notes on the information given.

Athens

Government. In ancient Greece, Athens was a monarchy, ruled by one king. In time, the nobles were depended on more and more to help defend the land and they began to demand more power in return. By the end of the Dark Ages, an oligarchy developed with power in the hands of a few. As the population grew in this society where much of the land was unsuitable for farming, food shortages occurred and people began to look for change. After a period of tyranny, an early form of democracy appeared, around 510 B.C. The entire process took several centuries. The democracy included a council of 500 who were chosen at random each year. The council proposed new laws and were paid for their service. An assembly included all citizens and met every nine days to vote on laws. Courts were composed of citizens who were paid to serve as jurors.

Economy. The main activity in the Athens area was farming. Most citizens had just enough land to support their families. The wealthy few had estates with slaves. Some tenant farmers rented land. Until 500 B.C. trading depended on bartering; around 570 B.C. the government began to make gold and silver coins. By 600 B.C., Athens had become an international trade center. The monetary system and trade led to wealth, but the wealthy were expected to give large sums of money to the government to support projects resulting in a flow of money back to the citizens.

Education. Boys from wealthy families began their formal education at age seven. They lived at home, unlike the Spartans. They were taught reading, writing, math, poetry, music, dance, and athletics. They had a much more liberal education than did the Spartans. At age eighteen, boys joined the army for two years of military service. For the wealthy, there were academies that allowed them to study throughout their lives. Girls received no formal education in Athens.

Lifestyle. Boys were more prized than were girls. Upon birth, infant girls were sometimes left abandoned outside the city gates. Men managed farms and estates and participated in government. Boys lived at home during their schooling. Girls received no training and often were married by age fifteen. Women cared for the home and raised the children. Athenians enjoyed greater freedom than did the Spartans and entertained themselves with myths, plays, and poetry.

Sparta

Government. The government of Sparta began as a monarchy with two kings and gradually moved toward an oligarchy with power in the hands of a few. The thirty-member Senate was composed of men over the age of sixty. The senators were elected by the citizens, who were male landowners over the age of thirty. Members of the citizen's assembly could not propose laws but could vote yes or no on the laws proposed by the senate or the ephors. The senate and the ephors really had the power to ignore a vote if they chose and power was concentrated in the hands of a few families.

Economy. Sparta had a military economy and Spartan men were required by law to be soldiers. As a result, people in the surrounding communities provided trade and craft items, although luxury goods were forbidden. Every citizen was given a plot of land by the government, and helots (state slaves) were assigned to farm the land. The helots were given crops as payment. The owner was required to give the government crops in exchange for daily meals; if he was unable to do so, he lost his rights as a citizen.

Education. Since Sparta was a militaristic city-state, education focused on military training, athletics (jumping, running, boxing, and wrestling), discipline, reading, and writing. At age seven, boys left their families to live in military barracks. Conditions in school were very harsh, since it was believed that hardship would create stronger character.

Lifestyle. Much can be understood by knowing that government inspectors were sent upon the birth of a child to determine whether the child would live or be abandoned in a cave to die. Male children lived in barracks from the age of seven and by age eighteen were expected to devote their lives to the army. At the age of thirty they gained full citizenship but were expected, even if married, to eat all meals with the soldiers in the mess hall. It can be inferred from this that family life was not nearly as strongly valued as was military life. Entertainment consisted of religious festivals, chorus contests, and dance contests.

Figure 5.11　Teacher Information Sheet on Athens and Sparta

Closure

"What were some ways that Sparta and Athens differed? How might we account for these differences? Where would you rather live, Sparta or Athens?"

Evaluation

Students complete self-assessments and group assessments (Figure 5.12) on their presentations. The teacher evaluates the presentations with respect to content accuracy and completeness. The teacher information sheet (Figure 5.11) can be used as one resource.

Extension Activities

1. Students create murals based on their research topics.
2. Students hold a debate based on the final closure question: Where would you rather live, Athens or Sparta?

Unit Self-Assessment and Group Assessment

Please evaluate your contributions to your group by placing an X at the location that most accurately reflects your own performance.

1. While creating the group banner, I did not take part

took responsibility for some part of the project

1   2   3   4   5

2. During the paper column experiment, I did not work cooperatively or share with others

worked cooperatively with others

1   2   3   4   5

3. When working with my group, I usually failed to stay on task

worked to the best of my ability

1   2   3   4   5

4. In a few sentences, explain what you enjoyed most about the Ancient Greece unit.

5. Which activity did you like the least? Why?

6. List some problems you and your group experienced while working on the assigned projects.

7. List some successes you and your group enjoyed while working on the assigned projects.

Additional Extension Activities

1. Arts/Banners. Have students create banners to hang from the ceiling over their groups. Each group decides on an appropriate name for their group and creates a banner made of butcher paper that depicts objects, mythological characters, architecture, or some other symbolism from ancient Greece. The members of each group must research their topic cooperatively and come to a meeting of the minds before the banner is begun.

D Rather than having students create a banner or a crayon relief, the teacher may prefer to have students research banners and their use or the procedures used to create vases.

2. Art/Vases for Folders. Have students create a crayon relief to decorate the covers of their folders.

a. Students cover a sheet of white paper with shapes of color.
b. They then color over the top with black crayon.
c. This is cut into the shape of a vase.
d. Students then illustrate their myths (from Lesson 4) by scraping away the black crayon with a paper clip to reveal the bright colors underneath, thus creating a crayon relief.
e. The vase is then fastened to the front of their folders with masking tape behind it, creating a three-dimensional effect.

3. Math. Give students a conceptual understanding of the Pythagorean Theorem by illustrating it using Cuisenaire materials. Introduce additional early concepts in geometry.

Additional Resources

Other CD-ROM and laser disc resources include:

- *World History Illustrated: Ancient Greece* (by Queue, for grades 6–12, CD-ROM for Mac or IBM)
- *Early Civilizations* (by BFA, for grades 4–12, laserdisc or VHS videotape)
- *Ancient Lands* (by Microsoft, for grades 5–12, CD-ROM for Mac or Windows)
- *The Story of Civilization* (by Compton's/World Library, for grades 7–12, CD-ROM for IBM & Windows)
- *Recess in Greece* (by Electronic Arts/Morgan Interactive, for grades 5–10, CD-ROM for MacIntosh)
- *History of Civilization* (by Queue, for grades 8–12, CD-ROM for IBM)

For younger children (grades 4–8), special education, and ESL students, as well as for independent reading, see *Favorite Greek Myths*, a Scholastic Smart Book (Scholastic), by Mary Pope Osborne, with illustrations by Mary Howell, on CD-ROM for MacIntosh computers. Available from Educational Software Institute, 4213 South 94th Street, Omaha, NE 68127.

For use with older students, grades 9 and up, consider using *Theseus: Caught in the Maze of Minos* (Compton's New Media/Westwind), a CD-ROM for MacIntosh computers. With this CD-ROM students can experience the fun and fascination of mythological lore as they follow the adventures of Theseus and his encounters with dozens of authentic characters. The program's giant database allows students to summon accurate information on gods, goddesses, and heroes and to quickly hunt down detailed maps and genealogical charts. This in-depth study of Greek literature, history and foreign culture tells the tales of gods and heroes with illustrations, narration, music, and sound effects. Requires Macintosh System 7.0 or greater and color. Available from Educational Software Institute, 4213 South 94th Street, Omaha, NE 68127.

Ancient Greek Unit Test

1. Compare the Olympic games in Ancient Greece to the games held today. How are they alike? How are they different?
2. Write the letter of the correct definition on the line after each vocabulary word.

    oligarchy   _____   a. rule by a few people
    barter   _____   b. independent self-governing unit
    helot   _____   c. government by the people
    sanctuary   _____   d. state slave
    democracy   _____   e. sad story of a flawed hero
    city-state   _____   f. a sacred place to honor gods
    monarchy   _____   g. rule by a king
    tragedy   _____   h. exchange one product for another

3. How did the geography of Greece affect (choose any two and explain)
    a. farming
    b. the development of city-states
    c. trade
    d. culture

4. We learned that there were four classes of people in Ancient Athens. What type of people belonged to each class and what rights did people of each class have?
5. Compare life in Athens to life in Sparta. Outline the differences. Where would you rather live? Why?

Figure 5.13 Unit Assessment Checklist to Be Kept in Student's Folder

Unit Assessment Checklist		
Item	Point Value	Student Self-Evaluation
Write your own myth	10	_____
Myth checklist (you are the reviewer)	5	_____
Group banner with a clear theme	5	_____
Vocabulary scribble	5	_____
Definitions and illustrations	5	_____
Retrieval chart (geography)	10	_____
Participation in games day	10	_____
Discus bar graph	10	_____
Paper column experiment	10	_____
Retrieval chart (levels of Greek society)	10	_____
Debate (knowledgeable participation)	10	_____
Self-assessment and group assessment	10	_____
Total	100	_____

Sample ITU 2: Early English Explorers and Settlers in North America

Middle and Secondary Grades. This ITU about early English explorers and settlers in North America can be adapted for students in middle and secondary schools. It is part of a social studies program about the development of the United States. Through selected learning materials, the students will develop a better understanding of the United States as they study about people with different backgrounds, different ideas, and different ways of life. In this unit, the students become better acquainted with the early explorers, the study of the early settlement of the colonies, the people who lived there, and some of the reasons they came to North America. The teacher can guide students as they compare that time period with present-day events, developing new insights about newcomers then and newcomers in the United States today.

General Goals

This unit is designed to explore

- Selected early explorers
- The early settlement of the colonies, the people who lived there, and some of the reasons why they came to North America.
- The effects of the environment on the people and their food, clothing, and shelter.
- How the idea of colonization then differs from the idea of colonization today.

> **M** A teacher's responsibility is to ensure that the thematic instruction incorporates the school, district, and state's frameworks, content and skill-related goals, and objectives for the grade level.

Unit Summary

Time Line. This unit was designed for ten days as part of a social studies program about the development of the United States of America.

Assessment. Individual learning of the students is assessed through teacher observation, portfolios, journals, and student participation in the collaborative and cooperative activities. There is daily ongoing observation/assessment of the students' progress as well as a cumulative evaluation at the completion of all of the lessons.

Diversity. In many of the activities, the students work with partners to complete the activities. ESL students are assigned to work with students who have strong oral skills. When appropriate, selections of children's literature related to the unit that present children of different ethnic and cultural groups will be read aloud. Selections can be made from a favorite source, such as *Subject Guide to Children's Books in Print* or *Developing Multicultural Awareness through Children's Literature* by Patricia L. Roberts and Nancy L. Cecil (McFarland, 1993). For example, the teacher can read aloud *My Name Is Pocahontas* by William Accorsi (Holiday House, 1992), a fictionalized biography told by the princess that begins in her childhood. She tells of her friendship with Captain John Smith, her marriage to John Rolfe, and her trip to England as Rolfe's wife. Another read-aloud choice is *The Double Life of Pocahontas* by Jean Fritz (Putnam, 1983), a biography (for grades 4–8) that focuses on the role Pocahontas played in the events between two cultures.

D The more diverse the students, the greater the need for integrated curriculum and active learning with partners (Garcia, 1994).

The following are suggestions concerning individual differences related to enrichment reading:

* *Blind and visually impaired students* can be given Braille materials, talking books, raised relief maps, projection magnifiers, and large-type printed materials. For information about products, reports, films, and publications, write to the American Foundation for the Blind, Consumer Products Department, 15 West 16th Street, New York, NY 10011.
* *Deaf and hearing impaired students* can be provided with assistance from a parent or interpreter as needed, as well as the use of visuals and the overhead projector for questions and responses. For information and a catalog of products, write to Gallaudet University.
* *Language minority students* can be provided with bilingual materials as needed and when desired, bicultural material. Write to National Clearinghouse for Bilingual Education, 1300 Wilson Boulevard, Suite B2-11, Rosslyn, VA 22209 and Gryphon House, 3706 Otis House, P.O. Box 217, Mount Ranier, MD 20822 (multiethnic books).
* *Less-able students* can be provided with easy-to-read books, shown filmstrips, given brief assignments, and assigned to cooperative learning groups. To inquire about materials for learning disabled and educable mentally retarded persons, write to C. C. Publications, Inc., P. O. Box 23699, Tigard, OR 97223.
* *Physically impaired students* can be provided with a buddy system to assist them in use of reference materials as well as other equipment and resources. To inquire about reading programs, write to the National Library Service for the Blind and Physically Handicapped, Library of Congress, Washington DC 20542 and to Telesensory Systems, Inc., 3408 Hillview Avenue, P. O. Box 10099, Palo Alto, CA 94304.
* *Regular-education students* can be provided with books to read and other resources to respond to questions recorded in a unit study guide.
* *Gifted students* can be given extensive reading related to the diversity of heritages from a unit bibliography that leads to class reports, independent inquiry, and biographical research about such persons as Sir George Carteret, Pocahontas, Squanto, Peter Stuyvesant, John Winthrop, and others.

* *
# LESSON 1
* *

Successful and Unsuccessful Explorations

Unit Guiding Questions

In what ways were explorers/settlers successful? Unsuccessful?

Lesson Question

In what way was acquiring food part of the success of an exploration?

Materials

Samples of edible plants/foods unique and unfamiliar to the students, ordered from a local producer.

Introduction

After a review of some information about some early explorers who traveled to North America, introduce the students to a simulation activity in which they take the roles of explorers who have the responsibility of finding some edible plants each day during an exploration.

Procedure

1. With the students in small groups, review the need for explorers to find food each day during a simulated activity.
2. Distribute some unfamiliar edible foods to the groups, such as watercress leaves, cilantro, ugli fruit (also called star fruit), raddicio, and so on. Ask the students to simulate finding these items. The students take the role of explorers who have not seen the foods before and are concerned about eating the foods. What would they do?
3. The students in groups engage in making decisions about the safety of eating the foods and discuss what they would do. Back in the whole class, a reporter from each group tells of the group's decisions. The decisions are written on the writing board or on an overhead transparency.
4. The decisions are discussed (e.g., don't eat the unfamiliar food; take a risk and eat the food item; test it in some way before eating it). Ask the students to brainstorm ways that explorers could have "tested" the food to determine it safe for human consumption.

D Effective instructional conversation (building on what others say so each statement expands, clarifies, or challenges previous statements) has been demonstrated as highly relevant to the linguistic, cognitive, and academic development of linguistically and culturally diverse students (Tharp & Gallimore, 1988, 1989; Tharp, 1989).

M/D Students can work in small groups designed to support their understanding of a particular concept of subject area.

Assessment

Teacher observation and monitoring of the students' participation in group work, in the discussion and in participating in decision making.

Additional Interdisciplinary Feature: Clarifying Terms

1. During group work, the teacher listens for the use of specific terms that need to be clarified. "Gretchen, you mentioned that Sir Francis Drake was a "seadog." How does your textbook define *seadog*?" Gretchen is asked to read the definition in the glossary of the text. The teacher points out that the students can always define a term by reading the definition in a dictionary or glossary or by inferring the meaning from the context of the text. "But there are other ways to define a term. For example, we can define a term by demonstrating something about it. Who wants to define *seadog* by demonstrating something a seadog might do?" Student responses are elicited. "We can also define something by describing it. Who wants to define *seadog* by describing something about a seadog?" The students respond. "And then, we can define a word or term by displaying an illustration. Who will find a picture to help us define *seadog*?" There is a discussion about the pictures the students locate and the contribution of the pictures to the definition of the word.

2. The teacher elicits from the students the four major ways that a word or term can be defined and records their responses as a summary on the board.

3. With the students in the whole group, the teacher asks them to consider the reasons that early explorers journeyed to North America and generalize, "Considering your reasons and our reading about the explorers, would you say the early explorers were successful or unsuccessful in starting colonies in North America?" In the discussion, the teacher asks students to clarify and define some of the terms they use and to support their opinions with evidence from their reading.

M Teachers can structure learning around selected skills or content components in ad hoc student groups for special assistance (Garcia, 1994).

•••••••••••••••••••••••••••••••••••••••

LESSON 2

•••••••••••••••••••••••••••••••••••••••

Problems in the Colonies

Unit Guiding Question

What can we learn about the problems the early English settlers had?

Lesson Question

What was needed to establish a successful colony?

Introduction

Drawings of early settlers' established colonies are displayed. "In our study today, we want to consider one of the first permanent settlements and some of the problems the settlers encountered. Then, in a 'settler's journal,' we can write our own version of what life was like for a day—the problems and the successes.

Procedure

1. After observing the filmstrip *The Pilgrims of Plimoth* by Marcia Sewall (Weston Woods, Weston, CT), the students brainstorm some of the Pilgrims' problems and successes, which are written in a list on the board.

2. The teacher reviews the list and has students help classify similar problems together under student-selected headings, such as Problems of Shelter and Problems Getting Food. Students also classify successes. The teacher asks the students to rank the problems and successes, with the greatest problem or success (from the students' point of view) as number one and so on. The teacher asks the students to justify their choices for their rankings, and a discussion of the rank ordering and what was needed in a successful colony closes the lesson.

T Laserdisc: *The First Thanksgiving* (Clearvue/eav), grades 1–3; *Pilgrims at Plymouth* (Clearvue/eav), grades 4–6.

Assessment

After the students justify their choices for greatest hardship or success, they receive written feedback (agreement/disagreement) from a peer-partner. Teacher assessment is done by observing the students' participation in the various discussions.

M Class expectations, matters of misbehavior, and consequences can be established with student input through class meetings (Glasser, 1986).

Additional Interdisciplinary Features

Mathematics

- The students' rankings of their choices can be written on the board or on an overhead transparency and then tallied. The purpose of this collection of data and the information it presents can be discussed.

Music

- For those students interested in music, invite the students to sing several songs related to the time period. Also, display a long, maple fife banded with brass ferrules and invite an interested student to play several tunes of the times. Music for such tunes can be found in *Amy, Ben and Catalpa the Cat* by Alice S. Owens (Colonial Williamsburg Press, 1990), a story set in eighteenth century Williamsburg.

- Invite interested students to engage in independent reading with Blackwood's book *Beethoven* by A. Blackwood, *A Little Schubert* by M. B. Goffstein, and *The Boy Who Loved Music* by D. Lasker. Use a time line on a transparency to show the era in which each composer lived to connect the composers with American events in this period. Ask students to prepare drawings of a composer, play samples of musical scores, and write background facts on transparencies to introduce a favorite composer of the period to others in the class.

- Invite students to sing the Shaker abecedarium from *A Peaceful Kingdom* by the Provensons (Viking, 1976, all grades) to the tune of "The Alphabet Song." Sing other story-songs that have historical significance from *Pop! Goes the Weasel and Yankee Doodle: New York in 1776 and Today with Songs and Pictures* by Robert Quackenbush (Harper, 1976, all grades).

M Schools must find ways to schedule opportunities for teachers to work together and to provide longer blocks of time for students to pursue interdisciplinary projects (ASCD, 1995).

- -
LESSON 3
- -

More About the Beginnings of Selected Colonies

Unit Guiding Question

What are some specifics about the beginnings of some selected colonies?

Lesson Question

Which colonies are associated with settlers (or other groups) in North America?

Introduction

Students watch a filmstrip, educational movie, or video about the early colonists and then discuss the beginnings of early colonies.

Procedure

1. Have students in small groups organize and summarize the information they have gained.
2. Back in the whole group, place the students' information on an overhead transparency. It can be based on the format in Figure 5.14.
3. Ask students to return to their small groups and summarize what was discussed by considering the following questions:

   What reason(s) can you give for why the colonies of Rhode Island, Connecticut, and New Hampshire were started?

   Were the middle colonies started for the same or different reasons? How do you know?

   How were the southern colonies started?

   What main idea or statement can your group make from this information?

4. In the whole group, have students report on the main idea or statement from each group.

Assessment

After the students report on the main idea or statement from each group, they receive written feedback (agreement/disagreement) from a peer in another group. Teacher assessment is based on the students' responses to the summary sheet and the way(s) they organize and summarize information in the small groups.

T Video: *Colonial Williamsburg* (Videotours, 1993), grades 7 and up. This documentary shows the physical development of the colony.

D Instructional conversation emphasizes the teacher's role in facilitating and guiding student learning through verbal interactions (Goldenberg, 1992).

T CD-ROM: *PilgrimQuest* (Decision Development Corporation), grades 4–12. This is an excellent multimedia resource.

To organize the material, scan your reading material, review your notes about the filmstrip, and recall what you learned from any group presentations. Blank space is provided for some of the information.

	Settler	Colony	Reason for Settling
1583	Sir Humphrey Gilbert		
1585	Sir Walter Raleigh		
1607	John Smith		
1620	Pilgrims		
1630	Puritans		
1681	William Penn		
1733	James Oglethorpe		

Figure 5.14 Format for Students' Organizing and Summarizing

```
• • • • • • • • • • • • • • • • • • • • • • • • • • • •
```
LESSON 4
```
• • • • • • • • • • • • • • • • • • • • • • • • • • • •
```

Information about the Colonies from Geography

Unit Guiding Questions

How did geography affect the colonies? What information about the colonies can be gathered from reading maps?

Lesson Question

What can we learn about the colonies from maps?

Procedure

1. In groups, students read text material or look at drawings or supplemental resources (maps) that relate to the setting of a selected colony.
2. Back in the whole class, have students brainstorm ways that the geography affected the colonies, such as their shelter, food (hunting, farming, gathering edible plants), clothing, work, recreation, trade, and contact with other cultures.
3. To summarize, students take roles as colonists and write an entry in their journals related to ways geography affected life in the colonies.

Assessment

Students self-assess their journal entries and decide whether to place it in the unit portfolio. The teacher assesses by observing students' participation in the group work and whole-class discussion.

Additional Interdisciplinary Feature

Mathematics and Science

- "Today, we are going to gather additional information about the colonies from reading maps. We will locate some major places and use the rulers to measure distances. We'll review map symbols to locate latitude lines and match a color code to locate specific colonies." With the students, distribute a worksheet similar to the one that follows to help them work on their maps skills. The teacher guides those students who need assistance as they respond to a worksheet similar to the Figure 5.15. Teacher assessment of this mini-lesson is based on an assessment of the students' responses to the worksheet and on the way(s) they demonstrate that they can locate places, determine distance, identify latitude, and read map symbols and color codes.

T Laserdisc: *The Geography of the New England States* (SVE), grades 4–8. This could be useful for both teacher and students.

T Laserdisc: *Map Skills for Beginners* and *Map Skills* (Coronet/MTI), grades K–5 and 3–6, respectively; *Latitude and Longitude* (National Geographic), grades 4–9.

T Software: *National Inspirer* and *Geography Search* (Tom Snyder Productions), grades 4–12 and 5–9, respectively.

M Journals provide opportunities for personal reflection, expression, and organization of thoughts (Gibbs and Earley, 1994).

D Vocabulary words for this activity will vary depending on the grade level, English language skill, and intellectual maturity of the students.

M The teacher may prefer to teach selected skills, such as map skills, in mini-lessons for ad hoc groups as a break-out instructional technique.

Map Skill for Individual Student Activity

Student _____ Date _____

Teacher _____ Period _____

Map I

Find the map on page _____ of your textbook. Complete the following items:

1. Locate the English colony of Roanoke Island. Write the name of the ocean that surrounds the island.
   _____

2. Calculate the miles to the inch with your ruler and measure the distance from the colony on Roanoke Island across the ocean to Raleigh Bay.

Map II

Find the map on page _____ of your textbook. Complete the following items.

3. Locate the colony on Roanoke Island again. Between which two lines of latitude was this colony located? _____ and _____

4. Study the map symbols to find out which group had the rights to the land where this colony started.

Map III

Find the map on page _____ of your textbook. Complete the following items.

5. Review the color code on the map and write the names of the colonies that were known as the New England Colonies.

   _____

6. Which colonies were known as the Middle Colonies?

7. Which colonies were known as the Southern Colonies?

Figure 5.15   Map Skills Worksheet

· ·
LESSONS 9 AND 10
· ·

Talking About What Was Learned

Unit Guiding Questions

What information about early English explorers and settlers and the colonies was learned?

Lesson Question

What did we learn about the early English explorers and settlers and the colonies?

Introduction

In small groups, students prepare for a culminating quiz show presentation. They discuss what they learned about the early English explorers and settlers and the colonies and review any materials they need, such as journal entries, self-assessment paragraphs, and so on.

D The more diverse the students, the greater the need for integrated curriculum and active learning with partners and small groups (Garcia, 1994).

Procedure

1. Preparing for the quiz show, the students develop clues about persons, places, and events related to the unit.
2. In a quiz-show format, the students take turns describing or giving clues about a particular person, place, or event related to the unit.

Assessment

Teacher assessment is based on the students' participation in group work. As the teacher meets with groups and observes, he or she makes notes on adhesive-backed note papers and later affixes those notes to a checklist for each student. A sample checklist might look like Figure 5.16. Teacher assessment also is based on the students' responses to the quiz show and the way(s) they demonstrate that they can share information about the topic.

A Diversity of Heritages: Sample of Unit Bibliography

African Heritage

Petry, A. *Tituba of Salem Village*. HarperCollins, 1991. Tituba, an intelligent black slave is vulnerable to suspicion and attack from the witch-hunters in Salem. Historical fiction. Grades 5 and up.

T CD-ROM: *Black American History: Slavery to Civil Rights* (Queue Inc., 1994), grades 7 and up.

Figure 5.16 An Assessment Checklist for an Individual Student

Assessing a Student in Group Work			
Student _____		Date _____	
Teacher _____		Period _____	
The student participated in:	**Often**	**Sometimes**	**Seldom**
the task of the group			
helping others			
decision-making			
discussing information			
organizing information			
drawing conclusion(s)			
preparing materials to present findings			
discussing positive contributions of others			
making a positive contribution to the group			
other as determined by the teacher			

Asian Heritage

Namioka, L. *The Coming of the Bear*. HarperCollins, 1992. In the 1600s two samurai, Zenta and Matsuzo, escape to Ezo (now Hokkaido) and confront the warlike tension between the Aimu who live there and Japanese colonists who are trying to settle on the island. The two solve the mystery of a bear that keeps attacking the settlers during the winter, easing the tensions of war. Historical fiction. Grades 5–9.

European Heritage

Anderson, J. *The First Thanksgiving Feast*. Ill. by G. Ancona. Clarion, 1989. Anderson gives first-person accounts of life at Plymouth in 1620s. The photographs are taken at Plimouth Plantation, a Living History Museum. Nonfiction. Grades 3–6.

Asimov, I. *Henry Hudson*. Gareth Stevens, 1991. Henry Hudson (?–1611), a British sea captain, is sent on the *Hopewell* by the English Muscovy Company in 1607 to find a passage to the east around North America. The book focuses on Hudson's voyages, his crew, and the trouble he has. In 1609, the East India Company hires him to search for a northwest passage, and in his ship, the *Half Moon*, he enters the now–Hudson River and sails as far as today's Albany, New York. On a similar voyage in 1611, the crew mutinies and places Hudson, his son, and loyal sailors adrift in a small boat and they are never heard from again. Labeled drawings of Hudson's ships and a glossary are included. Grades 3–4.

Bulla, C. *A Lion to Guard Us*. Crowell, 1981. Three motherless London children sail to Jamestown to find their father in the new colony. When the ship is wrecked in a storm near Bermuda, the children save their lion's-head door knocker. They survive on the island until another ship is built to take them to Virginia. There, they find their father, one of the few who survives the Starving Time in 1609. Young Jenny hangs the lion's head on a peg above the door latch, a symbol of their former home. Fiction. Grades 3–4.

Hunter, M. *You Never Knew Her as I Did*! HarperCollins, 1981. Will, a young page at Lochleven Castle, writes his memoirs of 1542–1587 about Mary, Queen of Scots. Historical fiction. Grades 7 and up.

Kagan, M. *Vision in the sky: New Haven's Early Years 1638–1783*. Shoe String, 1989. Kagan presents aspects of colonial life with a focus on the strict Puritan values they live by and their relations with Native Americans. They give up security and comfort for their hopes. The book ends with the defeat of the British Redcoats in the Revolutionary War. Nonfiction. Grades 4–8.

Kurelek, W., and Engelhart, M. *They Sought a New World: The Story of European Immigration to North America*. Tundra Books, 1985. This book depicts the various groups of people who settled on the North American land. Nonfiction. Grades 4 and up.

Monjo, F. N. *The Secret of the Sachem's Tree*. Dell, 1973. Ill. by M. Tomes. This is the story of the people who hide the Connecticut charter in an oak tree in 1667 to keep the charter from being returned to England. The work is based on historical facts. Fiction. Grades 1–5.

D Minority children are affirmed by seeing members of their ethnic or linguistic groups pictured or described in literature (Ross, 1993). Note the story of Japanese colonists in the 1600s in *The Coming of the Bear*.

M Teachers should select books that are well written, emphasize human relations, and cause the reader to consider the actions of characters (Gibbs & Earley, 1994).

Quackenbush, R. *Old Silver Legs Takes Over: A Story of Peter Stuyvesant*. Prentice Hall, 1986. This portrays the life of Stuyvesant, a colorful leader of New Amsterdam. Grades 1–5.

Rinaldi, A. *A Break with Charity: A Story about the Salem Witch Trials*. Harcourt Brace Jovanovich, 1992. In Salem, Susannah English wants to join the girls who meet to have their fortunes told by the slave Tituba. She observes the subsequent mass hysteria, through which people are named as witches, and finds the courage to help end the "crying out" that threatens to tear apart her community. Historical fiction. Grades 5–8.

Sewall, M. *The Pilgrims of Plimoth*. Macmillan Children's Group, 1986. This book is based on the writings of Governor William Bradford of the Plymouth Colony in 1620. It describes the lives and responsibilities of the children, women, and men who lived there. Nonfiction. Grades 4 and up.

Stanley, D., and P. Vennema. *Good Queen Bess: The Story of Elizabeth I of England*. Ill. by D. Stanley. Macmillan Children's Group, 1990. This portrays the life of Queen Elizabeth I (1533–1603) and her influence on religion, politics, and exploration of the New World. Biography. Grade 4.

Steck-Vaughn. *Rebellion's Song*. Author, 1990. This has six biographies about people of the Colonial Period. Grade 4.

Walters, K. *Samuel Eaton's Day: A Day in the Life of a Pilgrim Boy*. Scholastic, 1993. Set in 1627 at Plimouth Plantation, the book portrays a hard day in the life of seven-year-old Samuel as he gets dressed, checks his animal snare, and gathers wood before he eats his breakfast of curds, mussels, and parsley. During the day, he helps the men harvest rye despite the pain of his blisters. Historical fiction. Grades 2–6.

Hispanic Heritage

Chow, O., and Vidaure, M. *The Invisible Hunters*. Children's Book Pr., 1987. Portrays the impact of the first European traders on the life of the Miskiot Indians in 17th century Nicaragua. Historical fiction. Grades 4–7.

Marvin, I. R. *Shipwrecked on Padre Island*. Ill. by L. Miller. Hendrick-Long, 1993. Marooned in 1554, thirteen-year-old Catalina loses her bracelet, which is found 400 years later by thirteen-year-old Jilliane. Fiction. Grades 5–7.

Native American Heritage

Brebeuf, Father Jean de. *The Huron Carol*. Dutton, 1993. This is the story of the birth of Christ as set in the Huron world, written by a missionary, Father Jean de Brebeuf, in the 1600s. Folk literature. Grade 4.

Bulla, C. R. *Squanto, Friend of the Pilgrims*. Scholastic, 1990. This is the story of the life of the Native American who helped the European pilgrims survive in the New World. It portrays the assistance given by Squanto (*Tisqugntum*, ?–1662) to the pilgrims at Plymouth Colony. He teaches the Pilgrims the Indian way of planting corn and helps them survive their first winter in Plymouth. Biography. Grades 2–5.

M Teachers should select a highly motivational, well-written book that relates to the topic or issue to be studied and read it aloud in order to create interest and discussion that lead to further investigation (Ross, 1993).

T Video: *Catch the Whisper of the Wind* (Horizon 2000, 1993), grades 7 and up. This has quotations and songs of American Indians in tribal languages.

Fritz, J. *The Double Life of Pocahontas*. Ill. by E. Young. Putnam, 1983. This book details life of a Native American princess and her journey to England as the wife of John Rolfe. Biography. Grades 4–8.

Holler, A. *Pocahontas: Powhatan Peacemaker*. Chelsea, 1993. This book recounts life of Pocahontas and her role in helping the English survive at Jamestown. Biography. Grades 6 and up.

Kessel, J. K. *Squanto and the First Thanksgiving*. Ill. by L. Donze. Carolrhoda, 1983. Squanto, the last of the Paatuxet Indians, teaches the Pilgrims ways to survive the harsh winter in Massachusetts. Biography. Grade 4.

Sewall, M. *People of the Breaking Day*. Atheneum, 1990. This book portrays the Wampanoag people as a proud industrious nation in southeastern Massachusetts before the settlers arrived. Sewall shows the life in the tribe and the place of each member in the society, giving details about hunting, farming, survival skills, and the value of a harmonious relationship with nature. Includes recreational and spiritual activities. Nonfiction. Grades 4–5.

Differently Abled

De Trevino, E. B. *Nacar, The White Deer*. Farrar, Straus & Giroux, 1963. A mute Mexican shepherd boy protects a white deer and presents it to the King of Spain in 1630. Historical fiction. Grades 4–6.

Female Image

Christian, M. B. *Goody Sherman's Pig*. Macmillan, 1991. Goody Sherman in 1636 began a legal battle over her runaway pig with church elders and the courts. It was said that her battle caused the colony to create two legislative branches of government. The work is based on historical fact. Historical fiction. Grades 2–6.

Fradin, D. B. *Anne Hutchinson: Fighter for Religious Freedom*. Enslow, 1989. Anne Hutchinson (1591–1643) holds meetings in which she preaches that true religion is the following of God's guidance through an "Inner Light," without regard to the preachings of a church or minister. Later, in Massachusetts in 1638, Anne is put on trial for "traducing" the ministers, is found guilty, and ordered to leave the colony. Anne's family starts a settlement at Portsmouth that offers complete religious freedom for all, where she lives until moving to Pelham Bay, New York, where she is killed by Indians in 1643. Biography. Grades 5 and up.

IlgenFritz, E. *Anne Hutchinson*. Chelsea, 1991. Details Hutchinson's early life and gives an historical context for her banishment from the New England colony. Biography. Grades 5 and up.

Nichols, J. K. *A Matter of Conscience: The Trial of Anne Hutchinson*. Ill. by D. Krovatin. Steck-Vaughn, 1993. Nichols describes religious climate in which Hutchinson lived and mentions the difference between a "Covenant of Works" and a "Covenant of Grace," two views that help readers understand her words and actions before and after her trial. Biography. Grades 4–6.

T Video: *Masks of Culture* (New Dimensions Media, 1992), grades 8 and up. This documents the importance of masks of the Native American culture and their use in tribal ceremonies. *Squanto and the First Thanksgiving* (Rabbit Ears Prod./Listening Library, 1993), grades 5–6. Graham Greene, an Oneida Indian, narrates the story of Squanto.

D For a bibliography of titles relevant to the differently abled, see Friedberg, J. B., J. B. Mullins, and A. W. Sukiennik, *Portraying Persons with Disabilities: An Annotated Bibliography of Nonfiction for Children and Teenagers* (New York: Bowker, 1992).

D/T Taking an imaginary journey via literature, particularly historical fiction and biography, creates interest in distant lands and other time periods (Ross, 1993).

Speare, E. G. *The Witch of Blackbird Pond*. Houghton Mifflin, 1958. Kit, raised by a loving grandfather, is encouraged to read history, poetry, and plays. Historical fiction. Grades 7 and up.

Religious Minority

Aliki. *The Story of William Penn*. Prentice Hall, 1984. Quaker leader William Penn (1644–1718) establishes the colony of Pennsylvania as a refuge for religious nonconformers. He treats fairly the Indians who named him Onas, which meant quill or pen. Biography. Grades 4–6.

Ammon, R. *Growing Up Amish*. Macmillan Children's Group, 1989. This book portrays the history of the Amish movement and shows the Amish lifestyle in a Pennsylvania Dutch area. Nonfiction. Grades 3 and up.

Costabel, E. D. *The Jews of New Amsterdam*. Atheneum, 1988. Costabel recounts the struggles of the Jews who journeyed to America from Brazil during the colonial period and discovered that the United States did not hold equality for all its people. Nonfiction. Grades 4–5.

Rice, E. *American Saints and Seers: American-born Religions and the Genius Behind Them*. Four Winds, 1982. Rice describes America's various religions, including the Native American Indian religions, the Shakers, Mormons, and Christian Scientists. Nonfiction. Grades 7–8.

Sample ITU 3: Spring

(Kindergarten and First Grade)

Unit Summary

Time Line. The unit is designed for five days during the rainy season, with the first lesson scheduled after a rainstorm (or after creating teacher and student-made water puddles).

Assessment. Individual learning of the students is assessed through teacher observation and student participation in the activities. There is also daily ongoing assessment of the students' progress as well as a cumulative evaluation at the completion of all five lessons.

> **M** Class and student expectations, matters of misbehavior, and consequences can be established in class meetings (Glasser, 1986).

Materials

Lesson 1—water puddles, baggies, chalk, art paper, and crayons or makers.

Lesson 2—art paper, circles, scissors, printed leaves and stems, glue, seeds, soil, and cups.

Lesson 3—chart paper, pencils, colored markers or crayons, and art paper, rulers, microscopes or magnifying glasses, samples of tree pieces.

Lesson 4—earthworms in soil, spiders in jar, ant in ant farm, and miscellaneous objects such as seashells for counting.

Lesson 5—art paper, tempera paints, brushes, white construction paper 18 inches wide, sentence strips, and pocket chart.

Diversity. All students select partners with whom to complete the activities. ESL students are assigned to work with students who have strong oral skills. When appropriate, the teacher reads aloud selections of children's literature that present children of different ethnic and cultural groups. For example, the teacher might read aloud *Bringing the Rain to Kapiti Plain: A Nandi Tale* by Verna Aardema (Dial, 1981), an accumulating story from Kenya about the way a herdsman accepts his obligation to make things better for his people, the environment, and the animals.

> **D** Thonis (1983) points out that the following strategies help introduce nonreaders in their own language to reading in English: use of real experiences and real objects, talking about pictures, reading to students and demonstrating meaning, reciting poetry in choral groups, creating chart stories, playing word games, and making class dictionaries and word files.

Source: Unpublished work by Stephanie Carrington, Nancy Giboney, Suzanne Cantlay, and Kevin MacDonald. Reprinted by permission.

•••

LESSON 1

•••

Water and Puddles

Unit Guiding Questions

What are some of the connections among water, rain, and evaporation? What are some of the different aspects of water?

Lesson Question

What happens to water puddles over a period of time?

Introduction

After a rain storm, when the ground is wet with accessible water puddles (or after the teacher has sprayed water from a hose on an outside area), ask the students to cover their shoes with baggies and fasten the baggies around each ankle with a rubber band. Before going outside, discuss several questions with the students and write their responses (predictions, guesses, hunches) on the board to be reviewed and confirmed later:

* What do you think the water in the puddle will do when you walk through it? (spread out) Why do you think so?
* What do you think will happen when you walk away from the puddle? (make wet shoeprints) Why do you think this is so?
* Do you think the shoeprints will last forever? Why or why not?

Procedure

1. Have the students walk through the water puddles. Ask them to observe what happens to the puddles when they walk through them and what happens after they walk away from the puddles.
2. Distribute chalk pieces to each student and have them draw around the puddles so they can compare the sizes. Which is largest? Smallest? About the same?
3. With the students back in the classroom, point out the earlier responses (predictions, guesses, hunches) written on the board. Have the students check their predictions and confirm the appropriate ones.

M Active teaching can be utilized to foster students' engagement in the tasks, to promote student involvement, to pace instruction, and monitor student participation and progress (Tikunoff, 1983).

T CD/Audio Cassette: "When the Rain Comes Down" on *A Cathy and Marcy Collection for Kids* (Rounder Records, 1994), grades K–2.

4. Invite the students to draw two pictures—one showing what the puddle looked like when they walked through it outside and another showing what they think the puddle will look like in two hours.

5. After two hours, have students go outside to check the puddles and discuss what has happened. Point out that the puddles will eventually recede as they evaporate, becoming smaller and smaller until they dry up.

Assessment

The teacher assesses the students' pictures to determine the extent to which the students predicted a change in the puddle.

Additional Interdisciplinary Feature

Music

- Invite the students to sing several songs, including "If Only the Raindrops Were Lemon Drops" on *Raffi's Evergreen, Everblue*.

D Children can observe how weather changes through the year and draw conclusions about its effect on people's lives (Seefeldt, 1993).

T Audio Cassette: *Raffi's Evergreen, Everblue* (Troubador, 1990), grades K–2. This cassette includes environmental theme music.

D *We Are Better Together* (New Hope Records, 1994), grades K–3. This cassette includes repetitive songs of friendship.

LESSON 2

Flowers

Unit Guiding Question

How do flowers grow?

Lesson Question

What is needed for flower seeds to grow?

Introduction

Arrange examples of flowers placed in front of the students and invite them to touch and smell them.

Procedure

1. Show students different types of seeds. If desired, place the seeds on the stage of an overhead projector so students can discuss the different shapes and sizes.
2. Elicit from the students a point of view similar to that of a botanist. Ask what they think is important for seeds to grow and develop into flowers (soil, water, sunlight, wind, and other ways of seed dispersement).
3. Have students in small groups plant their own seeds so they can eventually observe the life phenomena exhibited by the plants (observations botanists use). Point out that since the seeds are all different, each student will eventually have a unique flower that can grow in their region (botanists are interested in plant life in various regions). Discuss the idea that the flower seeds depend on the students for care.

Assessment

The teacher monitors students' participation in discussion, planting seeds, and the eventual flowering of the seed.

Additional Interdisciplinary Feature

Art/Botany

- After students have planted the seeds, have them use scissors, glue, and art paper or printed leaves and stems to create their ideas of flowers, such as roses.

D Primary-grade students can increase their abilities to use their senses to gain information.

T Video: *Wonders of Growing Plants* (Churchill Media, 1993), grades K–4. Diverse children explore ways plants are propagated with seeds, cuttings, succulent leaves, and roots. *Look What I Grew: Windowsill Gardens* (Intervideo/Pacific Arts Video, 1992), grades K–4. This introduces students to hydroponics.

T Audio Cassette and Book: *Miss Rumphius* (Puffin Books, 1994), grades K–2. The primary theme is making the world beautiful.

D Active teaching behaviors include communicating directions clearly, presenting new information clearly, maintaining students' involvement in tasks, communicating expectations, and monitoring students' progress (Tikunoff, 1983).

```
•  •  •  •  •  •  •  •  •  •  •  •  •  •  •  •  •  •  •  •  •  •  •  •  •  •  •  •  •  •  •
```
LESSON 3
```
•  •  •  •  •  •  •  •  •  •  •  •  •  •  •  •  •  •  •  •  •  •  •  •  •  •  •  •  •  •  •
```

Trees in Bloom

Unit Guiding Question

What can we learn from observing trees?

Lesson Question

In what ways can we observe trees?

Introduction

Arrange parts of flowering trees such as almond and cherry in front of the students and invite them to touch, smell, and manipulate the parts.

Procedure

1. Before reading aloud Shel Silverstein's *The Giving Tree* (Harper-Collins, 1964), elicit students' thoughts about the title and some of the illustrations. Write the students' thoughts on the board. After reading the story aloud, discuss their initial thoughts and compare them with the story.
2. Explain that different types of trees do not produce leaves and flowers at the same time. Ask students why they think that leaves would develop at different times (temperature, sunlight, water, and other environmental conditions). Ask students these questions:

   Do you think that all the leaves come out at the same time on the same tree? Why or why not?

   Do you think that all trees produce flowers at the same time? Why or why not?

3. Invite the students to examine the pieces of trees native to the region. Show the shapes and sizes on the stage of an overhead projector.
4. Invite the students to draw what they have observed about trees on a section of paper.

Assessment

The teacher assessment is conducted by observing the students' drawings and assessing the participation in the discussion.

T Video: *My First Science Video* (Sony Kids' Video, 1992), grades K–4. This video is based on *My First Science Book* (Knopf, 1990), with fifteen easy science experiments, such as how colored water travels through stems into petals.

T/D CD-ROM: *A World of Plants* (National Geographic Society, 1993), grades K–3. This program offers nature study about the parts of a plant and topics of What Is a Seed?, A Tree through the Seasons, and Plants Are Important. Pronunciation and parts of speech are in English and Spanish. Spoken instructions are available in Spanish.

LESSON 4

Things That Creep and Crawl

Unit Guiding Question

What can we learn from observing different animals active in the springtime?

Lesson Question

What is needed to observe different animals active in spring? Why would it be important to be able to count the number of different animals?

Introduction

Act out the movements of different animals seen in the region in the springtime, such as ants, spiders, worms. Crawl through the classroom and ask students to predict the name of the animal. Exaggerate the motions and invite all students to join in.

Procedure

1. With students in small groups, distribute specimens in short, inexpensive plastic glasses. Then ask the students to observe and discuss the different creatures. Ask a student-facilitator in each group to pass around the earthworms and ants for the students to touch.
2. Back in the whole class after students have observed the animals, discuss such questions as:
   What do earthworms seem to do when they are returned to the soil? Why do you think they are doing this behavior?
   What do ants seem to do when they are returned to the soil?
   What do spiders seem to do when they are returned to the soil?
   What else do you want to know about these animals? How could you find out?

3. Invite the students to go outside with small shovels and dig for similar small animals to bring back to the classroom for display and discussion.
4. Invite the students to mention what they learned about animals that are seen in the springtime in their area and write their suggestions on the board.

T Software: *Science Starters* (Teacher Support Software, 1993), grades K–2. This program has story building through a writing program with pictures, word processing, and speech support around themes of Birds, Bugs, and Seasons.

M Class time can offer active learning activities that students pursue independently or with others (Garcia, 1994).

D Teachers can arrange the day so students work on group activities in small groups. Cross-cultural interactions take place when students work together to complete tasks (Garcia, 1994).

Assessment

The teacher assessment is conducted by circulating around the room and eliciting the students' responses. The teacher also observes student participation in the activities of the lesson.

Additional Interdisciplinary Feature

Mathematics

- The students are asked to practice their math skills by counting some of the ants, earthworms, and spiders. A study sheet can be designed with various numbers of animals, and the students are asked to use circular disks as counters (manipulatives) as they count.

● ●

LESSON 5

● ●

Rainbows

Unit Guiding Question

What can we learn from observing a rainbow?

Lesson Question

What are the different colors of a rainbow?

Introduction

Ask which students have ever seen a rainbow and what time of year they have seen a rainbow. Discuss the "prettiest" feature of a rainbow and review the names of the colors.

Procedure

1. With the whole class, discuss the seven primary colors found in a rainbow. Invite the students to paint rainbows by using the seven colors. Display the artwork in the classroom.
2. Read aloud lines on strips with sentences about the colors in the rainbow. For a second reading, invite the students to read along chorally. If desired, construct individual books using photocopied duplicates of the sentence strips.

Assessment

The teacher assessment is performed during the students' choral reading of the sentences and observation of the students' paper strip books of sentences.

Summary

Now that you have reviewed the three examples of the interdisciplinary thematic units, turn your attention to Exercise 5.1, Examining Units. The exercise is designed to help you refine and polish your own individual unit. You'll see various ways that the teachers have developed a unit for an integrated curriculum.

When you have completed the exercise, you might select further readings related to ITUs from the Suggested Readings. In addition, Turn to the appendix and Planning Master 8, "A Teacher's Checklist on Unit Development," to assess your reflections about what went into the development of your ITU for an integrated curriculum.

EXERCISE 5.1
Examining Units

• • • • • •

Instructions.   The purpose of this exercise is to examine selected instructional units—ones that are in this chapter, ones that have been supplied by your course instructor or another educator, or ones that you have borrowed from teachers in the elementary, middle, or high schools. In small groups, review each unit by identifying and discussing the features in the list below. Talk about the features in your small group, and then share information about the unit with your whole class.

1. Grade level and theme, main idea, topic, or guiding question being studied:

2. Time estimate for the unit:

3. Give examples in the unit of the following:
    Theme, main idea, topic, or guiding question(s)

Specific activities

Resources (materials and audiovisual needs)

Assessment procedures

4. What changes, if any, would you make in this unit? Why?

5. Features you would incorporate or not incorporate into your own teaching that you want to discuss.

Suggested Readings

Aschbacher, P. R. "Humanitas: A Thematic Curriculum." *Educational Leadership* 49, 2 (October, 1991): 16–9.

Association for Supervision and Curriculum Development (ASCD). "Refocusing the Curriculum: Making Interdisciplinary Efforts Work." *Education Update* 27 (January 1995): 1, 3, 7.

Barber, J., Bergman, L., and Sneider, C. *To Build a House: GEMS and the "Thematic Approach" to Teaching Science.* Berkeley, CA: Lawrence Hall of Science, 1991.

Barufaldi, J. O., Carnahan, P. S., and Rakow, S. J. *Texas Elementary Science Inservice Program.* Education for Economic Security Act Title II, Project 00690401-04. Austin, TX: Texas Education Agency, 1991.

Bates, E. *Language and Context: The Acquisition of Pragmatics.* New York: Academic Press, 1976.

Beyer, B. K. "Teaching Critical Thinking: A Direct Approach." *Social Education* 49 (April, 1985): 297–303.

Bloom, B. S., ed. *Taxonomy of Educational Objectives, Book I: Cognitive Domain.* White Plains, NY: Longman, 1984.

Brooks, J. G., and Brooks, M. G. *In Search for Understanding: The Case for Constructivist Classrooms.* Alexandria, VA: Association for Supervision and Curriculum Development, 1993.

Bruner, J. S. *Child's Talk: Learning to Use Language.* New York: Norton, 1983.

Bruner, J. S. *Actual Minds, Possible Worlds.* Cambridge: Cambridge University Press, 1986.

Caine, G., and Caine, R. N. "The Critical Need for Mental Model of Meaningful Learning." *California Catalyst* (Fall, 1993): 18–21.

Cecil, N. L., ed. *Literacy in the '90s: Reading in the Language Arts.* Dubuque, IA: Kendall/Hunt, 1990.

Cohen, E. *Student Influence in the Classroom.* Paper presented at the annual meeting of the American Educational Research Association, Toronto, 1978.

Cohen, E. *Status Equalization in the Desegregated School.* Paper presented at the annual meeting of the American Educational Research Association, San Francisco, 1979.

Cohen, E. *Continuing to Cooperate: Prerequisites for Persistence.* Bloomington, IN: Phi Delta Kappa Educational Foundation, 1990.

Cohen, E. G. *Designing Groupwork Strategies for the Heterogeneous Classroom.* New York: Teachers College Press, 1986.

Cohen, E., Lotan, R., and Catanzarite, L. "Treating Status Problems in the Cooperative Classroom." In *Cooperative Learning: Theory and Research,* edited by S. Sharon. New York: Praeger, 1984.

Cooper, R. D., and Odell, L. *Evaluating Writing.* Urbana, IL: National Council of Teachers of English, 1977.

Costa, A. L., ed. "Teacher Behaviors That Enable Student Thinking." In *Developing Minds: A*

Resource Book for Teaching Thinking. Alexandria, VA: Association for Supervision and Curriculum Development (1985): 125–37.

de Avila, R., Cohen, E., and Intili, J. K. *Multicultural Improvement of Cognitive Abilities*. Final report of Contract No. 9372. Sacramento, CA: State Department of Education. NIE Grant No. NIE-G-078-0958.

Dewey, J. *How We Think*. Boston: D. C. Heath, 1933.

Dreikurs, R. *Discipline Without Tears*. New York: Harper & Row, 1972.

Dwyer, C. *Language, Culture, and Writing*. Berkeley, CA: Center for the Study of Writing, University of California, 1991.

Everett, E. "Do the Write Thing," *The Science Teacher* 61, 7 (October, 1994): 35–7.

Gagne, R. M., Briggs, L., and Wager, W. *Principles of Instructional Design*. 3rd ed. New York: Holt, Rinehart & Winston, 1988.

Gamberg, R., Kiwak, W., Hutchings, M., and Altheim, J. *Learning and Loving It: Theme Studies in the Classroom*. Portsmouth, NH: Heinemann, 1988.

Garcia, E. *Understanding and Meeting the Challenge of Student Cultural Diversity*. Boston: Houghton Mifflin, 1994.

Gehrke, N. J. "Explorations of Teachers' Development of Integrative Curriculum." *Journal of Curriculum and Supervision* 6, 2 (Winter, 1992): 107–17.

Gere, A., editor. *Roots in the Sawdust: Writing to Learn Across the Disciplines*. Urbana, IL: National Council of Teachers of English, 1985.

Gibbs, L. J., and Earley, E. J. *Using Children's Literature to Develop Core Values*. Fastback 362. Bloomington, IN: Phi Delta Kappa Educational Foundation, 1994.

Ginott, H. G. *Teacher and Child*. Englewood Cliffs, NJ: Merrill/Prentice Hall, 1971.

Glasser, W. *Control Theory in the Classroom*. New York: Harper Collins, 1986.

Goldenberg, C. *Instructional Conversations and Their Classroom Application: Educational Practice Report # 2*. Santa Cruz, CA: National Center for Research on Cultural Diversity and Second Language Learning, University of California, 1992.

Goodman, K. S., Smith, E. B., Meredith, R., and Goodman, Y. *Language and Thinking in School*, 3rd Edition. New York: Richard C. Owen, 1987.

Grady, E. *The Portfolio Approach to Assessment*, Fastback 341. Bloomington, IN: Phi Delta Kappa Educational Foundation, 1992.

Hahn, M. L., and Goubeux, S. "Keepers of the Earth." In *SIGNAL*, Journal of the International Reading Association's Special Interest Group on Literature for the Adolescent Reader, 17, 4 (1993): 6–7.

Halliday, M. A. "Three Aspects of Children's Language Development: Learning Language, Learning through Language, and Learning about Language." In *Oral and Written Language Development through Research: Impact on the Schools*, edited by Y. Goodman, M. Haussler, and D. Strickland. Urbana, IL: National Council of Teachers of English, 1982.

Hancock, G. "Developing Children's Writing through a Thematic Approach." *Reading* 21, 3 (November, 1987): 185–204.

Harmin, M. *Inspiring Active Learning: A Handbook for Teachers*. Alexandria, VA: Association for Supervision and Curriculum Development, 1994.

Harrow, A. J. *Taxonomy of the Psychomotor Domain*. New York: Longman, 1977.

Hart, L. *Human Brain, Human Learning*. White Plains, NY: Longman, 1983.

Hartoonian, H. M., and Laughlin, M. A. "Designing a Social Studies Scope and Sequence for the 21st Century." *Social Education* 53 (October, 1989): 388–98.

Hickman, J., and Bishop, R. S. "African-Americans: Journey to Freedom." *The Web* 17 (2) (Winter 1993): 18–19.

Hill, D. "Order in the Classroom." *Teacher Magazine* 1, 7 (April, 1990): 70–7.

Hoskisson, K., and Tompkins, G. *Language Arts Content and Teaching Strategies*. Englewood Cliffs, NJ: Merrill/Prentice Hall, 1987.

Jacobs, H. H., and Borland, J. H. "The Interdisciplinary Concept Model: Theory and Practice." *Gifted Child Quarterly* 30 (Fall, 1994): 159–163.

Jacobs, H. H., et al. *Interdisciplinary Curriculum: Design and Implementation*. Alexandria, VA: Association for Supervision and Curriculum Development, 1989.

Jarolimek, J., and Foster, C. D., Sr. *Teaching and Learning in the Elementary School*. 5th ed. Englewood Cliffs, NJ: Merrill/Prentice Hall, 1993, pp. 149–153.

Kagan, J. Do Infants Think? *Scientific American* 2, 26: 74–82.

Kellough, R. D. *A Resource Guide for Teaching K–12*. Englewood Cliffs, NJ: Merrill/Prentice Hall, 1994.

Kellough, R. D., and Kellough, N. G. *Middle School Teaching: Methods and Resources*. 2nd ed. Englewood Cliffs, NJ: Merrill/Prentice Hall, 1996.

Kellough, R. D., and Roberts, P. L. *A Resource Guide for Elementary School Teaching: Planning for Competence.* 3rd ed. Englewood Cliffs, NJ: Merrill/Prentice Hall, 1994.

Kounin, J. S. *Discipline and Group Management in Classrooms.* New York: Holt, Rinehart & Winston, 1970.

Krathwohl, D. R., Bloom, B. S., and Masia, B. B. *Taxonomy of Educational Goals, Handbook 2, Affective Domain.* New York: David McKay, 1964.

Lee, S. *Bilingual-Bicultural Pedagogy: Integrating Korean Cultural Schemata into American Preschool-Kindergartens.* Doctoral dissertation, Southern Illinois University, 1989.

Lindfors, J. W. *Children's Language and Learning.* Englewood Cliffs, NJ: PrenticeHall, 1987.

Little, J. "Forum." *The Sacramento Bee,* 28 November 1993 (Sunday), p. 4.

Mah, D. "Bowling Green Charter School: A Story of Change." *Forward,* Newsletter for California Association for Supervision and Curriculum Development (January 1994): 5, 12.

Massialas, B. G. and Hurst, J. B. *Social Studies in a New Era.* New York: Longman, 1978. p. 27.

Moffett, J., and Wagner, B. J. *Student-centered Language Arts and Reading, K–13, 3rd. ed.* Boston: Houghton Mifflin, 1983.

Myers, J. W. *Making Sense of Whole Language.* Fastback 346. Bloomington, IN: Phi Delta Kappa Educational Foundation, 1993.

National Council for the Social Studies. *Social Studies Curriculum Planning Resources.* Dubuque, IA: Kendall/Hunt, 1990.

Newman, J. M., ed. *Whole Language Theory in Use.* Portsmouth, NH: Heinemann, 1985.

Richmond, G., and Striley, J. "An Integrated Approach." *The Science Teacher* 61, 7 (October, 1994): 42–45.

Roberts, P. L. *A Green Dinosaur Day: A Guide for Developing Thematic Units in Literature-Based Instruction, K–6.* Boston: Allyn & Bacon, 1993.

Roberts, P. L. *Literature-based History Activities for Children, Grades 4–8.* Needham Heights, MA: Allyn & Bacon, 1996.

Roberts, P. L. and Cecil, N. L. *Developing Multicultural Awareness through Children's Literature: A Guide for Teachers and Librarians, K–8.* Jefferson, NC: McFarland & Company, 1993.

Rosenblatt, L. M. *The Reader, the Text, the Poem: The Transactional Theory of Literary Work.* Carbondale, IL: Southern Illinois University Press, 1978.

Rosenblatt, L. M. *Literature as Exploration.* Urbana, IL: National Council of Teachers of English, 1983.

Ross, E. P. *Using Children's Literature Across the Curriculum.* Fastback 374. Bloomington, IN: Phi Delta Kappa Educational Foundation, 1994.

Seefeldt, C. *Social Studies for the Pre-School-Primary Child.* 4th ed. Englewood, Cliffs, NJ: Merrill/Prentice Hall, 1993.

Shoemaker, B. J. E. *Integrative Education: A Curriculum for the Twenty-First Century.* Eugene, OR: Oregon School Study Council, 1989.

Skinner, B. F. *The Technology of Teaching.* New York: Appleton-Century-Crofts, 1968.

Smith, F. "Demonstrations, Engagements, and Sensitivity: A Revised Approach to Language Learning." *Language Arts* 58 (January, 1981): 103–112.

Smith, F. *Essays into Literacy.* Portsmouth, NH: Heinemann, 1983.

Stenmark, J. K. *Assessment Alternatives in Mathematics: An Overview of Assessment Techniques That Promote Learning.* Berkeley, CA: Regents of the University of California, 1989.

Stevenson, C., and Carr, J. F., eds. *Integrated Studies in the Middle Grades.* New York: Teachers College Press, 1993.

Sun, T. "Charter Schools: Two Sacramento Schools Accept the Challenge." In *Forward,* Newsletter for California Association for Supervision and Curriculum Development (January, 1994): 5, 9, 10, 11.

Swartz, E., editor. "Thematic Instruction." *Communicator,* California Association for the Gifted, 21, 4 (September, 1991).

Switzer, S. "The Shuteyes." In *SIGNAL,* Journal of the International Reading Association's Special Interest Group on Literature for the Adolescent Reader, 17, 4 (1993): 3–5.

Texas Education Agency. *Writing Inservice Guide for English Language Arts and TAAS.* Austin, TX: Texas Education Agency, 1993.

Tharp, R. G., "Psychocultural Variables and K Constants: Effects on Teaching and Learning in Schools." *American Psychologist* 44 (1989): 349–59.

Tharp, R. G., and Gallimore, R. *Rousing Minds to Life: Teaching, Learning, and Schooling in Social Context.* Cambridge: Cambridge University Press, 1988.

Tharp, R. G. and Gallimore, R. *Challenging Cultural Minds.* Cambridge: Cambridge University Press, 1989.

Thonis, E. W. "The English-Spanish Connection." In *Excellence in English for Hispanic Children through Spanish Language and Literary Development.* Northvale, NJ: Santillana Pub. Co., 1983.

Tikunoff, W. J. *Compatibility of the SBIF Features with Other Research on Instruction of LEP Students.* SBIF-83-4.8-10. San Francisco: Far West Laboratory, 1983.

Trevarthan, C. "Descriptive Analyses of Infant Communication Behavior." In *Studies in Mother-Infant Interaction*, edited by H. R. Schaffer. London: Academic Press, 1979.

Villegas, A. M. *Culturally Responsive Pedagogy for the 1990s and Beyond.* Princeton, NJ: Educational Testing Service, 1991.

Vygotsky, L. S. *Mind in Society: The Development of Higher Psychological Processes.* Cambridge, MA: Harvard University Press, 1978.

Wee, Jan. "The Neshonoe Project: Profiles in Partnership." *World School for Adventure Learning Bulletin* (Fall, 1993): 2–3.

Wells, G. *Learning through Interaction: The Study of Language Development.* Cambridge, MA: Cambridge University Press, 1981.

Wells, G. *The Meaning Makers: Children Learning Language and Using Language to Learn.* Portsmouth, NH: Heinemann, 1986.

Williams, J., and Reynolds, T. D. "Courting Controversy: How to Build Interdisciplinary Units." *Educational Leadership* 50, 7 (April, 1993): 113–15.

Willis, S. "Choosing a Theme." *ASCD Curriculum Update.* Alexandria, VA: Association for Supervision and Curriculum Development (November, 1992): 4–5.

Willis, S. "Interdisciplinary Learning: Movement to Link Disciplines Gains Momentum." *ASCD Curriculum Update.* Alexandria, VA: Association for Supervision and Curriculum Development (November, 1992): 1.

Write More, Learn More: Writing across the Curriculum. Vol. 2. Bloomington, IN: Phi Delta Kappa, 1988.

Yorks, P. M. and Folio, E. J. "Engagement Rates during Thematic and Traditional Instruction." ED 363412 1993.

Appendix

Many teachers asked for duplicates of the exercises in this book related to developing an interdisciplinary thematic unit. Twenty-nine Planning Masters have been provided for this purpose on the following pages.

PLANNING MASTER 1: SCHEMA MAP

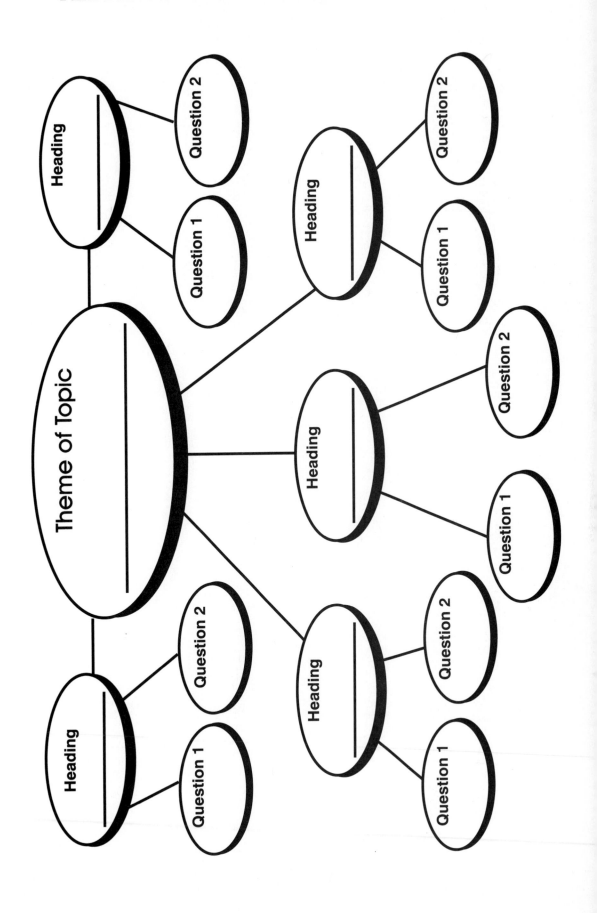

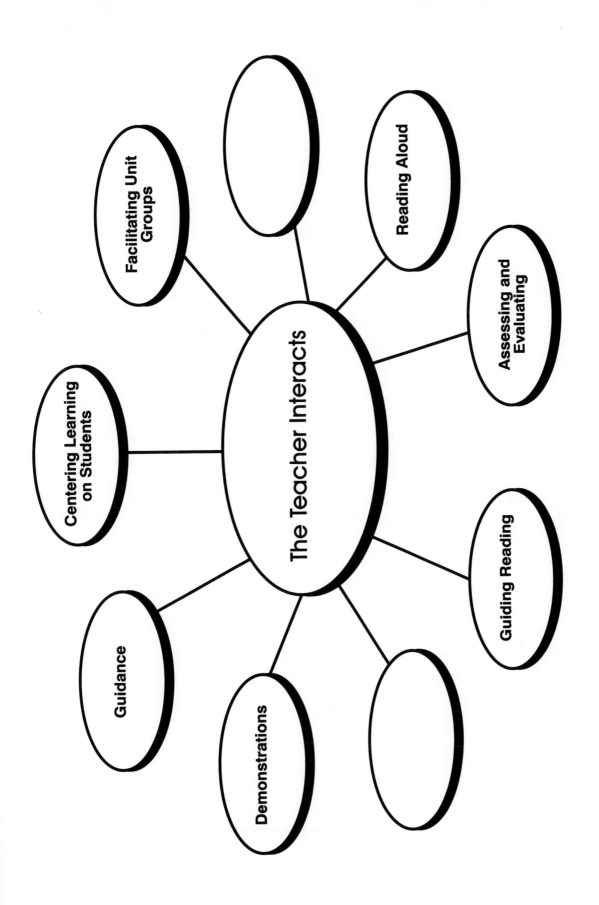

PLANNING MASTER 3: INTERACTIVE WEB FOR THE STUDENT

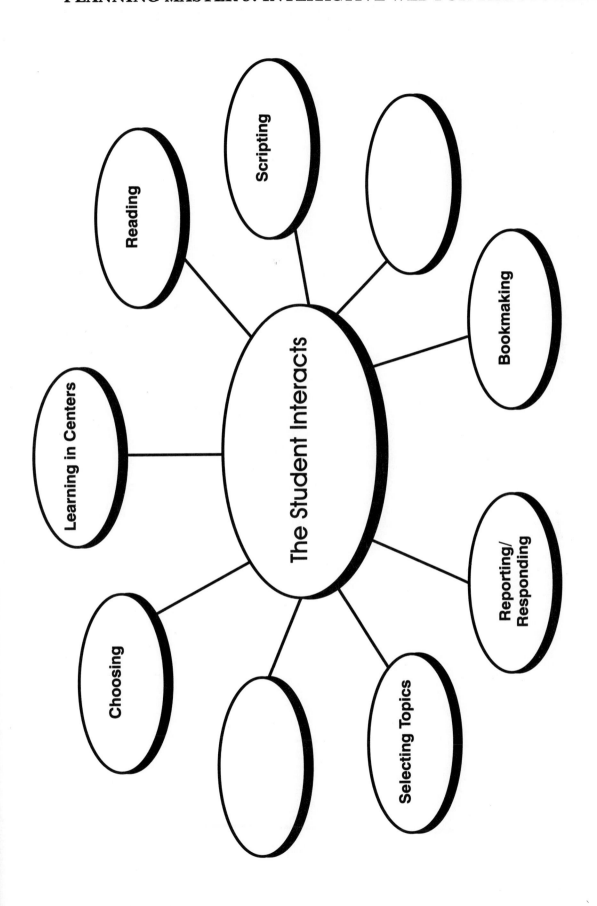

PLANNING MASTER 4: SELECTING A THEME

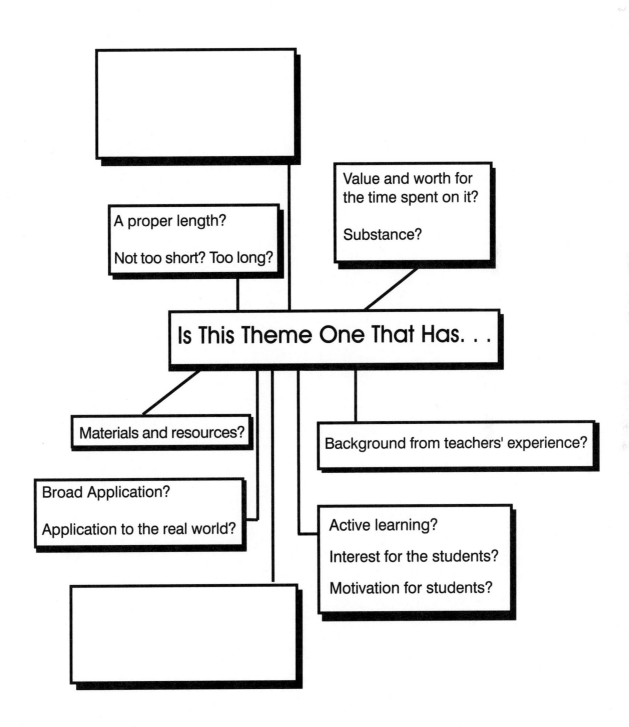

Value and worth for
the time spent on it?

Substance?

A proper length?

Not too short? Too long?

Is This Theme One That Has. . .

Materials and resources?

Background from teachers' experience?

Broad Application?

Application to the real world?

Active learning?

Interest for the students?

Motivation for students?

Planning a Field Trip Related to ITU

Purpose: _____

Trip Mechanics

Where we'll go:

Name of contact person:

Pre-trip visit by teacher:

Transportation plans:

Time to arrive/depart:

What students will need (lunch? appropriate clothing? money?):

Permission needed?

Adults who will be going:

Provisions for first aid:

Restroom location:

Student/Teacher Decisions

Pre-learning:

What do we want to find out?

Trip conduct:

Alternate plan for bad weather:

Introducing Students to Content Disciplines

Anthropology "How will our experience(s) in our own culture help us understand the way other people lived?" "What direct observations can we make to see a relationship about people's behavior and their beliefs?"

Economics "What work in the economy is done by people to develop and bring information to us?" "What economic problem(s) can be identified?" and "What resolutions of the problem(s) can be suggested?"

Expressive Arts "How can we show what we know about the subject through visual and performing arts, i.e., art, music, dance, sculpture, etc.?"

Geography "How has geography influenced the subject and what we know about the subject?"

History "How has this subject changed over time?" "How have ways we receive information about the subject changed over time?"

Mathematics "How can we express what we know about the subject through mathematics?"

Science "What life science, earth science, or physical science concepts connect to the topic?" "What scientists operate to bring us information about the subject?"

Political Science "How have people organized themselves to provide information about the subject?"

Sociology "What groups in society operate to bring us information about the subject?" "In what ways in the community can we participate to resolve a real problem related to the subject?"

Other Disciplines Selected by the students and the teacher.

Sample Checklist for Unit Assessment

Name of student _____ Date _____

1. Can identify theme, topic, main idea of the unit   _____

2. Can identify contributions of others to the theme   _____

3. Can identify problems related to the unit study   _____

4. Has developed skills in:
   - a. Application of information   _____
   - b. classifying   _____
   - c. categorizing   _____
   - d. decision-making   _____
   - e. discussion   _____
   - f. gathering resources   _____
   - g. justification of choices   _____
   - h. location of information   _____
   - i. organization of information   _____
   - j. reading text   _____
   - k. reading maps and globes   _____
   - l. reporting to others   _____
   - m. self-evaluation   _____
   - n. study habits   _____
   - o. summary preparation   _____
   - p. testing situations   _____
   - q. working with others   _____
   - r. working independently   _____
   - s. other features unique to the unit   _____

5. Overall view
   - a. demonstrates a sense of connectedness (deals with confusion and uncertainty and registers new insights; little evidence of downshifting)   _____
   - b. participated in authentic experiences   _____
   - c. involved in group participation   _____
   - d. involved in genuine community problem(s)   _____
   - e. engaged in the use of natural language   _____
   - f. positive peer relationships and other relationships   _____

Additional teacher comments:

A Teacher's Checklist on Unit Development

When developing an ITU for an integrated curriculum, I reflected upon related knowledge and skills:

Introduction to an Interdisciplinary Thematic Unit (Chapter 1)	Very Aware	Somewhat Aware	Need More
1. The Spectrum of Integrated Curriculum and where some of my own teaching efforts could be located on the spectrum.	_____	_____	_____
2. The theory that supports an integrated curriculum.	_____	_____	_____
3. A list of topics related to a unit theme.	_____	_____	_____
4. The purposes of an integrated curriculum.	_____	_____	_____
5. The interactions of the teacher that can be integrated into the unit.	_____	_____	_____
6. The interactions of the students that can be integrated into the unit.	_____	_____	_____
7. Ways to provide a multicultural perspective in the class.	_____	_____	_____
8. Needed instructional resources.	_____	_____	_____
9. Ways to use the community as an instructional resource.	_____	_____	_____
10. The arguments for/against the use of integrated curriculum.	_____	_____	_____
11. Information sources about ITUs.	_____	_____	_____
12. The interview with a teacher about the use of an ITU.	_____	_____	_____

Initiating an Interdiciplinary Thematic Unit (Chapter 2)

	Very Aware	Somewhat Aware	Need More
13. Working with others to select a theme.	_____	_____	_____
14. Investigating specific questions and selected resources to answer them.	_____	_____	_____
15. Identifying concepts and generalizations related to the theme.	_____	_____	_____
16. Identifying critical thinking processes used in selecting a theme and investigating questions.	_____	_____	_____
17. Selecting learning activities that are as direct and hands-on as possible.	_____	_____	_____
18. Incorporating major concepts & generalizations into a scope & sequence plan.	_____	_____	_____

Developing Objectives and Learning Activities (Chapter 3)	Very Aware	Somewhat Aware	Need More
19. Developing objectives.	____	____	____
20. Classifying objectives.	____	____	____
21. Developing learning activities.	____	____	____
22. Selecting a way to initiate an ITU.	____	____	____
23. Writing concepts and generalizations.	____	____	____
24. Developing a culminating activity.	____	____	____
25. Connecting questions and activities.	____	____	____
26. Doing personal inquiry.	____	____	____
27. Seeing objectives, resources and learning activities as a "whole."	____	____	____
28. Meeting needs and abilities of students.	____	____	____

Assessing and Evaluating (Chapter 4)

	Very Aware	Somewhat Aware	Need More
29. Ways to use measures of assessment (portfolios, anecdotal records, checklists, journals.	____	____	____
30. Developing a checklist for assessment.	____	____	____
31. Scheduling teacher-student conferences.	____	____	____
32. Selecting materials for student portfolios.	____	____	____
33. Ways to use a clearly established set of criteria that identifies differences in the students' achievement.	____	____	____
34. Ways to connect the portfolio with the report card.	____	____	____
35. Ways to asses the ITU with field testing.	____	____	____

Examining ITUs (Chapter 5)

	Very Aware	Somewhat Aware	Need More
36. Reading ITUs prepared by educators.	____	____	____
37. Ways to initiate an ITU.	____	____	____
38. Ways an ITU can include disciplines across the curriculum.	____	____	____
39. Ways teachers plan ITUs for different grade levels.	____	____	____

EXERCISE 1.2
Discovering Your Own Schema about an ITU

• • • • • •

Instructions: With others in a small group, brainstorm ideas related to an ITU and offer suggestions. Your purpose is to develop a list of topics related to a theme or topic of your choice. Remember, there are no right or wrong ideas—all are accepted. Consider the suggestions in the following web to keep the brainstorming going if the ideas "lag."

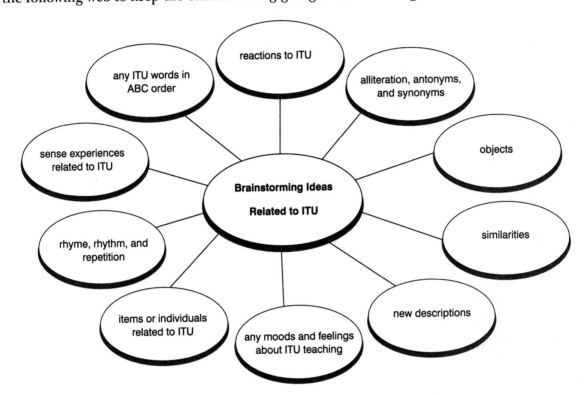

Involve two volunteers from the group to record your group's ideas on a chart or on a transparency that can be shown to others in the class on the overhead projector. You can organize the ideas in a web or another format as you wish. Follow these steps:

1. Suggest ways to categorize ideas about developing an ITU (i.e., what could be included) in categories and then suggest a theme and headings for the categories you see in the web in this exercise.

2. Individually, locate one professional article about an ITU and read it. Take notes.

3. Return to your small group and add any information to the web that you gained from the article.

4. Meet again with the whole group and report on the group's ideas about the ITU. Note the similarities and the differences in the schemata among the groups. Use the space on the next page for your notes (if needed).

EXERCISE 1.3

Discovering Informational Sources about ITUs

• • • • • •

Instructions: You have an important responsibility to be knowledgeable about an integrated curriculum before you develop an interdisciplinary thematic unit for your students. What informational sources stand out as useful ones in your mind? Your educational purpose for this exercise is to record some of the sources you can locate from your college studies that will help you to develop an ITU around a theme you have selected. Share what you have found with others in your class. One of your sources might be just the one someone else needs to develop and implement a unit.

(If you need assistance in locating a source that provides the information you want, select an entry from the Suggested Readings at the end of this book.)

1. Source:

Reason selected:

2. Source:

Reason selected:

3. Source:

Reason selected:

4. Source:

Reason selected:

5. Source:

Reason selected:

6. Source:

Reason selected:

7. Source:

Reason selected:

8. Source:

Reason selected:

PLANNING MASTER 12

EXERCISE 1.4
Interviewing a Teacher about ITUs

• • • • • •

Instructions: For this exercise, interview one or more elementary, middle, or high school teachers. Perhaps you will want to interview one who is new to the profession and then interview one who has been in teaching for five years or more. As an option, you may want to interview one who is teaching in elementary school and one who is teaching either at the middle school or high school. For this exercise, you may photocopy this form—one for each interview. Use the questions to guide the interview, and then report back to the whole group.

1. In what ways do you use interdisciplinary thematic units?

2. Why are you using (not using) interdisciplinary thematic units?

3. What training about interdisciplinary thematic units did you have?

4. What initial advice in terms of preparing an ITU can you offer me?

5. In what ways do you use resources in the community?

6. In what ways do you address the importance of diversity and multiculturalism in your classroom?

7. What do you like most about teaching with an ITU? the least?

8. What other specific advice do you have for those of us developing ITUs?

Other notes:

EXERCISE 2.1

Beginning an ITU: Selecting a Theme to Study, Formulating Questions, and Selecting Resources

• • • • • •

Instructions: The purpose of this exercise is to work with a parter or partners to gain insight into selecting a theme for an ITU. First, divide your class into partnerships representing elementary, middle, or high school interests and have two or more partnerships work together. Each group is to decide the grade level for which their ITU will be suitable.

1. If desired, simulate a cooperative group structure, assigning the following roles to members in each group of partnerships:

   Facilitator. Responsible for seeing that every member in the group gets the assistance that he or she needs.

   Checker. Responsible for seeing that every member finishes his or her work for the day.

   Reporter. Responsible for discussing what the group members learned during the ending debriefing session held each day after group work.

2. The first task is to select a theme for study, just as the students in your classroom could self-select their lines of inquiry.

   Theme:

What sources will you consult *before* you finally select a theme?

a. school, district, and state curriculum guides for your grade
   level   _____

b. student textbooks and teacher's manual for state adopted
   textbooks   _____

c. student interests and questions   _____

d. professional literature related to education   _____

e. other   _____

3. Working individually, brainstorm as many word and phrase associations about the group theme as possible. Write the theme in the center of the space below and group your associations around the theme (i.e., construct a web). Then show your work to others in your group.

(Theme)

4. Join a small group or the total group and contribute the word and phrase associations from step 3 to the common sharing of ideas. Have a volunteer write everyone's ideas in the form of a graphic web, and then replicate the web in the space below. Take notes on any discussion about it. Keep the web for reference as you continue your study of ITUs.

(Theme)

5. Ask any questions you have related to any of the words and phrases on the web. Assist the group members as they classify all of the members' questions into categories. Draw lines to connect any related categories, and then label the categories with headings of your choice. Make a sketch of the categories and their labels in the space that follows:

EXERCISE 2.2

*Beginning an ITU: Investigating Specific Questions and Identifying
Selected Resources*

• • • • • •

Instructions: The purpose of this exercise is to develop your skills in investigating specific questions and in selecting resources related to an ITU. For this exercise, use the theme and questions your group developed in Exercise 2.1.

1. From Exercise 2.1, select three (or more) questions about the group's theme that you would like to investigate.

   a.

   b.

   c.

   Other:

2. Now focus on the interdisciplinary aspect of the unit by writing questions about the theme from the perspective of people from various disciplines. You might begin with the disciplines that are closely related to your theme. Ask yourself, "What would an anthropologist want to know about this theme? an artist? a biologist? an historian? a mathematician? a sociologist? Writing these questions will help you determine how many subject areas you will incorporate in your thematic unit—a great many subject areas or just a few? Consult with others in your class if necessary.

Questions that could be asked by:
an anthropologist

an artist

a biologist

an historian

a mathematician

a sociologist

a writer/author

others

3. Reread your questions and underline words that represent concepts to be learned. What generalizations (big ideas) related to the theme can be written related to the thematic study?

4. Select one or more of your generalizations. Then look at the student textbooks, teachers' manuals, and curriculum guidelines for your grade to see if your generalizations can be taught through a topic identified in any of these resources. What did you discover?

5. For each question that you selected for further study (Step 1), identify the resources you could or would consult to investigate the question further. Resources can range from meeting resource people to reading printed material.

EXERCISE 2.3

Beginning an ITU: Identifying Critical Thinking Processes

• • • • • •

Instructions: The purpose of this exercise is to develop your skills in identifying the critical thinking you used in Exercises 2.1 and 2.2. In this exercise, you will review the steps you did in the previous two exercises and identify the critical thinking that each step required of you.

The specific intellectual processes used in this exercise were derived from Benjamin S. Bloom's *Taxonomy of Educational Objectives, Book I: Cognitive Domain* (1984). Bloom's taxonomy arranges intellectual processes from the simplest to the most complex in six categories— knowledge, comprehension, application, analysis, synthesis, and evaluation.

1. By referring to the steps in the previous exercises, think of an example of how you used each of the intellectual processes listed below. For each of your examples, briefly describe the way in which you engaged in that type of critical thinking.

   Knowledge (listing, naming, telling, defining, recording, labeling, collecting, specifying, enumerating). When did you recognize and recall information?

   Comprehension (recognizing, locating, retelling, identifying, restating, describing, explaining, reporting, translating, summarizing). When did you understand the meaning of the information you received?

   Application (showing, illustrating, practicing, exhibiting, demonstrating, dramatizing, simulating, calculating, applying). When did you use any of the information you received?

   Analysis (comparing, contrasting, arranging, organizing, diagramming, grouping, questioning, interpreting, inquiring). When did you use your ability to dissect information into component parts and see relationships?

Synthesis (assembling, constructing, creating, inventing, predicting, producing, developing, originating, hypothesizing, incorporating). When did you put components together to form a new idea?

Evaluation (measuring, estimating, criticizing, recommending, judging, revising, choosing). When did you judge the worth of an idea, notion, theory, thesis, proposition, or opinion?

2. Your purpose in the first three exercises of this chapter has been to gain insight into an interdisciplinary thematic unit of study. Now that you have completed the exercises, what insight(s) about starting an interdisciplinary thematic unit of study have you gained? Discuss this with others.

EXERCISE 2.4

Making Some Decisions Early: More about Scope and Sequence

• • • • • •

Instructions: The purpose of this exercise is to begin planning the scope and sequence of your interdisciplinary thematic unit. In your ITU plan, you want to incorporate the major concepts and generalizations that are in the curriculum guide for your grade level, as well as the ones you identified in Exercise 2.2. You also need to make various decisions about grouping, unit length, unit structure, and disciplines to be included.

1. *Individual Work and Group Work.* You might plan to have all types of grouping in your thematic unit. For example, you could begin each day or period with a whole-group discussion about the theme and then have students work with partners or in small groups. As an alternative, you could invite students to participate in a whole-group study of the theme and then ask students to request—and thus "reserve"—one area of study for individual inquiry. Decisions you want to make about individual work and group work:

2. *Length of Study.* Your unit can be of varying lengths. You might develop an ITU for a two-week grading period or a six-week grading period. You might plan four separate ITUs during the entire year, or you might plan another length of your choice. Decisions about length of study:

PLANNING MASTER 16 (*continued*)

3. *Concentrated Structure, Expanded Structure.* You might decide on an expanded structure, where the students have common experiences in a whole group situation, and then have students select separate areas of study to explore as individual or small-groups inquiries. On the other hand, you could decide on a concentrated structure, where the students learn mainly in whole-group situations with some partnership and small-group work. With a concentrated structure, the students realize the ITU has a beginning and an end. Decisions about structure:

4. *Disciplines to Include.* You might want to include a great many subject areas or just a few. Decisions about disciplines:

EXERCISE 2.5

Developing a Scope and Sequence for Initial Weekly Plans for an Interdisciplinary Thematic Unit

• • • • • •

Instructions: The purpose of this exercise is to develop the scope and sequence of an interdisciplinary thematic unit of study. For the purposes of this exercise, assume that you are interested in planning a three-week unit. Work with a partner or small group as you plan.

1. Select one of your generalizations related to your theme (Exercise 2.2, step 3) and write it in the appropriate space that follows. Review the students' texts to determine the extent of any material related to the thematic study. Write the page numbers or chapter numbers from the texts for future reference. If different generalizations are to be the foci of the other remaining weeks, review the texts for the material related to those generalizations, too.

Theme:

First Week

Generalization/overall question to focus on (underline words that reflect concepts):

	Science	Social Sciences	Expressive Arts	Math
Pages/chapters				
Ways teacher gives input				
Ways students give input				

Second Week
Generalization/overall guiding question to focus on (underline words that reflect concepts):

	Science	*Social Sciences*	*Expressive Arts*	*Math*
Pages/chapters				
Ways teacher gives input:				
Ways students give input				

Third Week
Generalization/overall guiding question to focus on (underline words that reflect concepts):

	Science	*Social Sciences*	*Expressive Arts*	*Math*
Pages/chapters				
Ways teacher gives input				
Ways students give input				

PLANNING MASTER 17 (*continued*)

2. If your ITU is planned for longer than three weeks, develop further your initial weekly plans in a format similar to the first three.

3. What plans do you have for your students to take an active part in the development of the thematic unit? (*Examples:* developing a question map; reserving a particular question for individual inquiry; suggesting resources and references to search for information; naming community resources; hands-on activities, small group work; whole gourp instructional conversations)

PLANNING MASTER 18

EXERCISE 3.1

Classifying Cognitive Objectives—A Self-check Exercise

• • • • • •

Instructions: The purpose of this exercise is to assess your ability to classify cognitive objectives. For each of the following cognitive objectives, identify by the appropriate letter the highest level of operation involved: K = knowledge, C = comprehension, AP = application, AN = analysis, S = synthesis, and E = evaluation. Check your answers, and then discuss the results with your peers. Your understanding of the concept involved is more important than whether your score is 100 percent.

_____ 1. Given a poem, the student will recognize the style as being that of Shelley.

_____ 2. Given a list, the student will recognize the misspelled words.

_____ 3. After reading detailed instructions, the student will participate and make a hand puppet.

_____ 4. The student will create a verse using a four-line stanza.

_____ 5. The student will explain his/her critical appraisal of an essay on civil rights.

_____ 6. The student will correctly identify by name the colors shown.

_____ 7. The student will be able to interpret faulty logic in campaign advertising.

_____ 8. Given the political and economic facts, the student will identify a reasonable hypothesis concerning the causes of the riots in Los Angeles.

_____ 9. The student will devise a method to prove that a ray bisects an angle.

_____ 10. Given a list of five solids, five liquids, and five gases, the student will describe the physical and chemical properties of each.

Answer Key

1. C		6. K	
2. K		7. E	
3. AP		8. AN	
4. S		9. S	
5. E		10. K	

EXERCISE 3.2

Initiating an ITU with a Question Map

• • • • • •

Instructions: The purpose of this exercise is to work with a partner or partners to write questions related to a theme you identified in Chapter 2.

   With your partners taking the role of students, have your partners participate in a discussion about "what we want to know" about the theme. Write their questions on a question map on the writing board. Show the partners how you can group their related questions (main questions and subquestions) together. Ask them to think of headings for the different categories of related questions. Use the following format for recording the input:

1. Theme:

2. Main question:

3. Related subquestions:

   a.

   b.

   c.

Copy the question map from the board to this page so you can use it as a reference.

EXERCISE 3.3

Developing Generalizations

• • • • • •

Instructions: The purpose of this exercise is to work with a partner or partners to identify concepts and write generalizations from the questions and subquestions generated in Exercise 3.1.

1. Ask your partners to take the role of students. Read each of their questions again, underlining the words in each that identify a concept that will need to be reinforced in your teaching. Have your partners participate in a discussion about any generalizations they can determine from the main concept words. Write the generalizations below:

2. With your partners, read each generalization again, underlining words in each that identify a concept that will need to be reinforced in your teaching. Select one or more of the concepts and discuss ways you can reinforce the concept in your teaching.

EXERCISE 3.4

Connecting Questions and Activities for an ITU

• • • • • •

Instructions: The purpose of this exercise is to work to connect the questions related to your theme and to learning activities in specific detail. Learning activities should be planned around some central questions (and subquestions) about the theme. The investigative activities that are needed to inquire about the questions can provide various opportunities for you to respond to the learning styles and needs of your students.

   With your partners, return to the "what we want to know" question map you completed in Exercise 3.2. Use the information to design some learning activities for the unit. (Figure 1.4 in Chapter 1 shows examples of questions and related activities.)

List of Learning Activities Related to the Questions and Subquestions

1.

2.

3.

4.

5.

6.

PLANNING MASTER 22

EXERCISE 3.5

*Personal Inquiry—Using Questions and Resources
and Recording Data*

• • • • • •

Instructions: The purpose of this exercise is to help you clarify your own concept of inquiry. In this exercise you will locate resources related to the main question and subquestions you developed in Exercise 3.2 and then record relevant data in those resources.

1. Take the role of a student in your classroom engaged in independent inquiry. Reread your question and subquestions, and then list any resources that you think will help you answer those questions. *Resources:*

2. Select one (or more) of the questions and collect information from the resources you listed to help you answer the question(s) you wrote related to your thematic study. Begin your search by consulting the sources you listed. Then consult other sources you find in the process.

3. Keep a record of your personal inquiry (as you might ask students in your class to do) by recording the information you find, your interpretations of the information, and the sources that verify your information.

Theme Study

Question 1:

Information Found

Interpretation

Source Used

Question 2:

Information Found

Interpretation

Source Used

Question 3:

Information Found

Interpretation

Source Used

Question 4:

Information Found

Interpretation

Source Used

4. What new questions came to mind as you collected information from the resources? Record any new questions, as well as any hunches, guesses, or predictions you have about the question(s) and the theme of the study.

New Questions:

Hunches, Guesses, Predictions:

5. With your partner(s), discuss your new questions and your hunches, guesses, and predictions.

PLANNING MASTER 24 (*continued*)

Feedback:

1. What was the reaction of your peer to your teaching plan?

2. In your opinion, did your plan convey what you originally envisioned?

3. What new questions came to mind as you wrote the plan?

EXERCISE 3.8

Planning Culminating Activities

· · · · · ·

Instructions: The purpose of this exercise is to plan a closure for the unit (even though you realize that inquiry can be life long and has no official closure). In this exercise, you must determine what will affect the length of your unit—the interest of your students in the topic, the resources that are available or unavailable, the school holidays, the academic calendar for your school year, and any competing events, such as picture day, assemblies and athletic events, and field trips.

1. What activity/activities could you plan that would permit your students to synthesize what they have learned in the unit and then report the synthesis to a selected audience?

2. Which of the following would you incorporate into the culmination of a unit? Explain why.

Creating new problems related to the topic and demonstrating a way to resolve them. Demonstrating computer software related to the topic.

Designing a chart, map, time line, classroom museum of exhibits, an interdisciplinary thematic fair, or a classroom "main street" with booths (learning centers), and reporting on the data the design represents.

Making an oral presentation on an aspect of the topic; using such creative ways to present data as sketches, sculpture works, cartoons, popular songs, a comic strip format, costume props, a story board, puppets, flannel board figures, rhymes, limericks, and other forms of poetry.

Producing an act in a play, a musical composition, or new lyrics for a familiar tune.

Reporting on interviews with other people.

Writing a letter or entries in a learning log or educational diary.

Writing a report related to the topic.

Writing and publishing a newsletter or brochure on the topic.

Writing and publishing an individual book.

Writing and publishing a cooperative-group book.

Writing and publishing a whole group book.

Writing and publishing a scientific article.

EXERCISE 3.9

Identifying Intellectual Processes, Disciplines, and Learning Styles of Students in the Learning Activities

• • • • • •

Instructions: The purpose of this exercise is to review your learning activities in more specific detail. In Exercise 3.4, you were asked to plan your learning activities around some central questions (and subquestions) about the theme. The activities that were needed to inquire about the questions can provide various opportunities for you to identify the related intellectual processes, discipline and subject areas, and the learning styles and needs of your students.

1. Return to the learning activities you wrote in Exercise 3.4 and identify the intellectual processes in the cognitive domain—knowledge, comprehension, application, analysis, synthesis, and evaluation—that are mainly emphasized in each activity. Identify these critical-thinking processes by abbreviations used in Exercise 3.1.

2. Review the learning activities again and identify the disciplines emphasized in each activity.

3. Return to your learning activities again and identify the learning styles of students emphasized in each activity. Identify these by the abbreviations of these learning styles:

sy for the word, **symbolic emphasis**, which indicates the activities ask students to think with symbol systems such as words and numerals; **im** for imaging which indicates the activities ask students to learn through visual or kinesthetic approaches; and **af** which indicates the activities incorporate feelings and emotions that could motivate students' inquiries.

4. Give your list of learning activities to another member in your class and ask him or her to review the identifications you made for each activity to see if you have addressed a variety of intellectual processes, disciplines, and learning styles to meet the needs of your students.

EXERCISE 4.1

Developing a Checklist for Assessment

. . . . . .

Instructions: The purpose of this exercise is to develop your skill in composing a checklist that would be useful in recording your notes as your observe students. Consider the arrangement of a general checklist form that follows, and then make your own improvements for a checklist you would use in your classroom.

Student _____   Grade _____   School _____

Teacher _____   Date _____   Period _____

   Expected Outcomes (Objectives)   *Students' Behavior*

1.

2.

3.

Teacher's Comments

EXERCISE 4.2
Assessment through the Use of Portfolios
• • • • • •

Instructions: The purpose of this exercise is to explore one way of assessing your students' learning as they participate in their inquiries through an interdisciplinary thematic unit. Portfolios are quite useful in assessing the students' progress because the teacher can collect information over the length of the unit. You should encourage the students to use their portfolios as a repository for their work—especially for their best work— and for descriptions or drawings of what they did (how they learned) that will show or describe the processes in which they were engaged.

Now explore your own understanding of portfolios by answering the following questions.

1. What materials do you think should be included in a student's portfolio that will show that the student has gained some relevant information related to the topic?

2. What materials do you think should be included in a student's portfolio that will show that the student has developed and used various thinking processes (observing, classifying, etc.) related to the topic?

3. What materials do you think should be included in a student's portfolio that will show that the student has used a variety of resources in his or her inquiry?

4. Reread what you wrote in earlier exercises about the learning activities that you would want to include in an interdisciplinary thematic unit and determine what materials would be produced from those activities. Which of the materials would you want placed in a portfolio?

EXERCISE 5.1
Examining Units

• • • • • •

Instructions: The purpose of this exercise is to examine selected instructional units—ones that are in this chapter, ones that have been supplied by your course instructor or another educator, or ones that you have borrowed from teachers in the elementary, middle, or high schools. In small groups, review each unit by identifying and discussing the features in the list below. Talk about the features in your small group, and then share information about the unit with your whole class.

1. Grade level and theme, main idea, topic, or guiding question being studied:

2. Time estimate for the unit:

3. Give examples in the unit of the following:

    Theme, main idea, topic, or guiding question(s)

    Specific activities

    Resources (materials and audiovisual needs)

    Assessment procedures

4. What changes, if any, would you make in this unit? Why?

5. Features you would incorporate or not incorporate into your own teaching that you want to discuss.

Children's Book Index

Name Index

Subject Index